REFLECTIONS OF NAZISM

Also by Saul Friedländer

PIUS XII AND THE THIRD REICH

PRELUDE TO DOWNFALL: HITLER AND THE UNITED STATES,
   1939–1941

KURT GERSTEIN: THE AMBIGUITY OF GOOD

ARABS & ISRAELIS: A DIALOGUE (WITH MAHMOUD HUSSEIN)

HISTORY AND PSYCHOANALYSIS

WHEN MEMORY COMES

REFLECTIONS OF NAZISM

An Essay on Kitsch and Death

SAUL FRIEDLÄNDER

Translated from the French by Thomas Weyr

1817

HARPER & ROW, PUBLISHERS, New York

Cambridge, Philadelphia, San Francisco, London

Mexico City, São Paulo, Sydney

Permissions acknowledgments appear on page 143.

This work was first published in France under the title *Reflets du Nazisme*.
© Éditions du Seuil, 1982.

FIRST EDITION

Designer: C. Linda Dingler

Library of Congress Cataloging in Publication Data

Friedländer, Saul, 1932-
  Reflections of Nazism.

  1. National socialism.   I. Title
DD256.5.F7413   1984   943.086   82-48117
ISBN 0-06-015097-1

84 85 86 87 88 10 9 8 7 6 5 4 3 2 1

Author's Note

The present translation of this book is a slightly revised version of the French original. The changes consist of some comments expanding on various points as well as a number of additional references.

Gentlemen, in a hundred years still another color film will portray the terrible days we are undergoing now. Do you want to play a role in that film which will let you live again in a hundred years? Every one of you has the opportunity today to choose the person he wishes to be in a hundred years. I can assure you that it will be a tremendous film, exciting and beautiful, and worth holding steady for. Don't give up!

Goebbels in 1945, discussing the film Kolberg

INTRODUCTION

On December 28, 1948, Albert Speer noted in his prison journal that the American publisher Blanche Knopf, who was interested in the publication of his memoirs, had written that "if we will have to wait too long, perhaps the material will not have the same importance it had months back."[1]* Twenty years later Speer's memoirs were a huge success. And all through the years, since the end of the war, Nazism was and remains the focus of the same fascinated interest. Thousands of books, dozens of films, and any number of articles have dealt with the topic. More than thirty-five years after it disappeared, the Third Reich remains the key reference point of contemporary history. For millions it is an unassimilated and unassimilable and yet changing reality.

At the end of the war, Nazism was the damned part of Western civilization, the symbol of evil. Everything

*Source notes begin on page 137.

the Nazis had done was condemned, whatever they touched defiled; a seemingly indelible stain darkened the German past, while preceding centuries were scrutinized for the origins of this monstrous development. A sizable portion of the European elites, who two or three years before the German defeat had made no secret of their sympathy for the new order, were struck dumb and suffered total amnesia. Evidence of adherence, of enthusiasms shared, the written and oral record of four years of coexistence with it, and indeed of collaboration, often vanished. From one day to the next, the past was swept away, and it remained gone for the next twenty-five years.

By the end of the Sixties, however, the Nazi image in the West had begun to change. Not radically or across the board, but here and there, and on the right as well as the left, perceptibly and revealingly enough to allow one to speak of the existence of a new kind of discourse. In France, for example, at the same time that the film *The Sorrow and the Pity* marked a further stage in a more authentic perception of collaboration and of the Resistance, Michel Tournier's novel *The Ogre* appeared as one of the first major manifestations of this new discourse.

This book is, first of all, an attempt to grasp these manifestations and understand the logic of this transformation, this reelaboration. For a minority of little interest here, the transformation of the past is deliberate; for others, it is a free game of phantasms. (I will use this term here in its most general sense and not in its psychoanalytic meaning, as a description of free constructs of the imagination, of chimeras, if you will.) For still others—for those who perhaps matter the most—it is a desire to understand, or, perhaps, a form of exorcism. "Do we ever free ourselves from the oppressing evil of guilt if we do not penetrate to the core of the disease that wastes us?" Hans-Jürgen Syberberg asks in the introduction to the published text of *Hitler, a Film from Germany*. Although the intentions are varied, a structure common to the whole of this new discourse is apparent. By and large, the works selected here—from various countries, mostly Germany, Italy, and France—as illustrations of this reinterpretation have enjoyed great popularity, a measure of their true significance and the reason for analyzing them. Despite differences of national, political, or social background, the profound logic of the changes they expound allows for numerous points of contact among them.

Such an amalgam of nationalities might be acceptable, but what about the ideological and social one? There is a new discourse about Nazism on the right as well as on the left. There is also an aesthetic reelaboration that goes beyond ideology. Can these varied approaches be considered as a whole? At one and the same time, can one move from political pamphlet to film, from film to novel, from novel to historical work, without changing tone and register? In short, can one deal with Michel Tournier, Hans-Jürgen Syberberg, and Albert Speer all at once?

One can, but not without explanation, and so a brief detour is needed. My point of departure is simple: It seems to me that any analysis of Nazism based only on political, economic, and social interpretations will not suffice. The inadequacies of the Marxist concept of "fascism," whether historical or contemporary fascism,

are obvious. But liberal historiography is no more coherent, and since the end of the Sixties, the key word
totalitarian arouses less and less interest. The structur-
al-functional approach seems an empty framework,
while psychohistorical analyses provoke a frequent
outcry. In short, the mountain of monographs that already obstructs the horizon cannot hide the theoretical
desert that stretches far into the distance.

Under the circumstances, only a synthesis of diverse
interpretations appears satisfactory: Nazism can thus
be seen as a product of a social and economic evolution
whose internal dynamic Marxism has perhaps il-
luminated; of a political transformation in part independent of the socioeconomic "infrastructure"; and, finally,
of a psychological process, responsive to its own logic,
that is intertwined with the economics and the politics.
Today the socioeconomic conditions needed for the appearance of a Nazi-type phenomenon do not exist, and
the political evolution of the West does not resemble in
the least that of Europe between the two world wars.

That leaves the psychological dimension, which,
being autonomous, followed its own course. It did not
rest on complex arguments nor sometimes on very clear
ideological positions. These evidently existed, but they
hid something else—an activity of the imagination that
cannot be reduced to the usual distinctions between
right and left. Nazism's attraction lay less in any explicit ideology than in the power of emotions, images, and
phantasms. Both left and right were susceptible to them
—at least during that crucial period from around 1930
until the German defeats midway through the war.

It seems logical, therefore, to suppose, a priori, that a

new discourse on Nazism will develop at the same level of phantasms, images, and emotions. More than ideological categories, it is a matter of rediscovering the durability of these deep-seated images, the structure of these phantasms common to both right and left. At that level, the works to be discussed lead independent lives in our imaginations as readers and viewers. Thus it does not matter whether Rainer Werner Fassbinder was a leftist, Joachim Fest is a right-wing liberal, and that Albert Speer may have altered his political convictions. What does matter, in Speer's memoirs, is the evocation of the night of August 23, 1939, when nature seemed to be in relationship to historical events; in *Lili Marleen,* the Führer symbolized as intense light; and in Fest's book, the meditation on Hitler's grandeur.

One can argue that the scene Speer describes is only one among many and should be put in its proper context; that the intense light in *Lili Marleen* is designed to enhance the film's irony; and that Fest's meditation on Hitler's grandeur is framed in the form of a question. It is equally arguable that Michel Tournier's fascinating portrait of Kaltenborn's SS prytaneum can be understood only within the general architecture of a work where the notion of "malignant inversion" plays a central role. Such objections would be valid if it were a matter of a test of intentions, a critique of attitudes, or the rendering of judgments. But my purpose, let me repeat, is different: In the first part of this essay, in any case, I shall trace associations of imagery, because I believe that these works, among others, carry within them a latent discourse ruled by a profound logic that needs to be clarified.

A word, too, about my criteria of selection. Given a discussion perceived essentially at the level of images and phantasms, why include George Steiner's *The Portage to San Cristóbal of A.H.*, which is basically a meditation on evil, while excluding Günter Grass's *The Tin Drum* (or, better yet, Volker Schlöndorff's film of it)? The Grass book, it seems to me, belongs to the previously usual forms of discourse about Nazism. Steiner's brief novel, on the other hand, does not.* As for the new discourse about Nazism, some aspects of it have already been noticed. In a review of Syberberg's Hitler movie, Nigel Andrews calls the way in which Hitler is turned into a part of the entertainment industry "a startling phenomenon of our times." He adds:

> The frequency with which Hitler and the Nazi era have been erupting onto our cinema screens, in the manifestations varying from the chamber melodrama of *Hitler—The Last Ten Days* to the Nazi chic of films like *Cabaret* and *Madam Kitty*, is, to say the least, curious. Should we hear in the sudden popularity of films about Hitler the healthy sound of skeletons being hauled out of closets, or the sinister strains of nostalgia for an age

*There are numerous studies of the expression or interpretation of Nazism, in all of its aspects, in modern literature, mostly in modern German or Jewish literature. See, among others, Lawrence L. Langer, *The Holocaust and the Literary Imagination* (New Haven: Yale University Press, 1975); Alvin H. Rosenfeld, *A Double Dying: Reflection on Holocaust Literature* (Bloomington: University of Indiana Press, 1980); Sidre Ezrahi, *By Words Alone: The Holocaust in Literature* (Chicago: University of Chicago Press, 1980); and Hamida Bosmajian, *Metaphors of Evil: Contemporary German Literature and the Shadow of Nazism* (Iowa City: University of Iowa Press, 1979). As for the treatment of Nazism and the Holocaust in film, see Annette Insdorf, *Indelible Shadows: Film and the Holocaust* (New York: Random House, 1983). The new discourse on Nazism, as defined here, is not the core problem of these studies.

when pageantry and patriotism and political certitude
reigned? Luchino Visconti's *The Damned* first glimpsed
the possibilities for a Grand Opera approach to the Nazi
era. And many of the more sumptuous movie treatments
of Nazi Germany have gone to the limits in matters of
pageantry and grand gesture and decorative finery. A
film like Tinto Brass's *Madam Kitty* comes closer to
Springtime for Hitler than to *The Damned,* though Visconti's film was clearly an influence. Likewise, *Cabaret*
derives most of its vitality not from the insipid love story
at the center but from the tangy, opulent corruption at
the edges.[2]

Andrews mentions some films that could have found
their place in this essay; on a different level—and seen
from a different angle—some of Werner Herzog's pro-
ductions could have been included, too. My aim, however, was not to write an exhaustive study of the subject but to use a few examples in order to uncover a
common structure of the new discourse. The examples
chosen are those I consider most typical: *Lili Marleen*
is more melodramatic than anything in the same line.
On the other hand, Herzog's avoidance of any direct
reference to Nazism would have created a major difficulty of interpretation; as for his murky mysticism and
his death and destruction themes, they appear no less
clearly in some of the major films mentioned in this
essay.

But these pages have a second aim, which, along the
way, has become their primary goal: An analysis of the
new discourse clearly shows that it is precisely this
reevocation and reinterpretation of the past that helps

17

us better to understand the past itself, especially in its psychological dimensions. Thus theme and aesthetics of *The Damned* and *Hitler, a Film from Germany,* for example, allow us to perceive something of the psychological hold Nazism had in its day. Thanks to their reflections in the present, some elements that a direct approach has not clarified up to now are revealed, *not so much by what this or that writer or director has intended to say, but by what they say unwittingly, even what is said despite them.* In effect, by granting a certain freedom to what is imagined, by accentuating the selection that is exercised by memory, a contemporary reelaboration presents the reality of the past in a way that sometimes reveals previously unsuspected aspects. It may help us to understand a fascination thus re-created, the elements of which seem to repeat themselves from one work to another. As a result of this kind of analysis, themes become visible, roads open up. The focus shifts from the new discourse about Nazism toward Nazism itself, and from Nazism back to the new discourse, allowing us to grasp some hidden forms of past and present imagination.

More precisely, beneath the visible themes one will discover the beginning of a frisson, the presence of a desire, the workings of an exorcism.

At the heart of each of the zones of meanings, profound contradictions emerge: an aesthetic frisson, created by the opposition between the harmony of kitsch (later I shall give a definition of the term *kitsch* as it will be used here) and the constant evocation of themes of death and destruction; a desire aroused by the eroticization of the Leader as Everyman, close to everyone's heart and of a total power of destruction flung into nothingness; an exorcism, finally, whose total endeavor, in the past and in the present, is—in the face of Nazi criminality and extermination policies—to maintain distance by means of language, to affirm the existence of another reality by inverting the signs of this one, and finally to appease by showing that all the chaos and horror is, after all, coherent and explainable.

In fact, an analysis of the new discourse, in revealing a deep structure based on the coexistence of the adoration of power with a dream of final explosion—the annulment of all power—puts us on the track of certain foundations of the psychological hold of Nazism itself, of a particular kind of bondage nourished by the simultaneous desires for absolute submission and total freedom.

Nazism has disappeared, but the obsession it represents for the contemporary imagination—as well as the birth of a new discourse that ceaselessly elaborates and reinterprets it—necessarily confronts us with this ultimate question: Is such attention fixed on the past only a gratuitous reverie, the attraction of spectacle, exorcism, or the result of a need to understand; or is it, again and still, an expression of profound fears and, on the part of some, mute yearnings as well?

I have already stressed that there is no question, in this essay, of condemning this or that attitude, this or that way of representing Nazism in the new discourse. My basic aim is to uncover some structures of the imagination, past and present. This being said, to pretend to be neutral would be hypocritical. The new discourse on

Nazism creates an uneasiness; one of the criteria that would allow many of us to recognize it immediately, prior to any analysis, is precisely this uneasiness. I know how imprecise this is, how different from one person to the other—in the case of Syberberg's movie, for instance, the opinions and feelings of people who certainly have no complacency toward a "new discourse" on Nazism are diametrically opposed—but still, when all the pieces mentioned in this essay as belonging to the new discourse are taken as a whole, the criterion of uneasiness is unmistakable. It stems, most of the time, from a dissonance between the declared moral and ideological position of the author or the filmmaker, the condemnation of Nazism and the will to understand and the aesthetic effect, be it literary or cinematographic (Nazism as an unlimited field for a surge of the imagination, for a use of aesthetic effects, for a demonstration of literary brilliance and the power of one's intellect. Hitler's final speech in George Steiner's novel and the play based on it is a classic example of what I have in mind). In her essay on Syberberg's *Hitler, a Film from Germany,* Susan Sontag writes:

> As the film is ending, Syberberg wants to produce yet another ravishing image. Even when the film is finally over, he still wants to say more, and adds postscripts: the Heine epigraph, the citation of Mogodishu-Stammheim, a final oracular Syberberg-sentence, one last evocation of the Grail. The film is itself the creation of a world, from which (one feels) its creator has the greatest difficulty in extricating himself as does the admiring

spectator; this exercise in the art of empathy produces a voluptuous anguish, an anxiety about concluding. . . .[3]

This is precisely the whole problem: Attention has gradually shifted from the reevocation of Nazism as such, from the horror and the pain—even if muted by time and transformed into subdued grief and endless meditation—to voluptuous anguish and ravishing images, images one would like to see going on forever. It may result in a masterpiece, but a masterpiece that, one may feel, is tuned to the wrong key; in the midst of meditation rises a suspicion of complacency. Some kind of limit has been overstepped and uneasiness appears: It is a sign of the new discourse.*

*Puzzlement sometimes replaces uneasiness, as when one discovers, for instance, the nature of a key idea that explains the main structure of Syberberg's film. Answering the question "Why make a seven-hour film on Hitler?" Syberberg states: "And—because Hitler was the greatest film maker of all times. He made the Second World War, like Nuremberg for Leni Riefensthal, in order to view the rushes privately every evening for himself, like King Ludwig attending a Wagner opera alone" (Steve Wasserman, "Interview with Hans-Jürgen Syberberg," *The Threepenny Review,* Summer 1980, p. 4). And from puzzlement back to uneasiness: "To make money with Hitler," declares Syberberg, "is not Nazism, but it is something similar. Hitler always said, 'they [the Jews] make money of everything.' People now make gold out of the ashes of Auschwitz. For example, the TV movie *Holocaust.* The same people: Jews who perhaps lost members of their family now make money out of the ashes of Auschwitz. How Goebbels would laugh! Of course, why not make money out of Auschwitz? Even a lot of Jews in Israel say, 'Why not? We are living in a free-enterprise system. We make money with everything. Why not with Auschwitz?' But what an idea! I can't. Maybe I am too German" (ibid., p. 5). In fact, in its more complex examples, the new discourse about Nazism is almost always a mixture of the three following levels of discourse: the language of images and the fascination it creates; strange statements—implicit in the works, explicit in interviews with the authors and directors—about history, modern civilization, the Nazis, the Jews, etc.; and an extremely sophisticated superstructure referring to metaphysics, theories of myth, the function of art and literature today, and so on. For an impressive example of what can be done at the superstructure level, see Thomas Elsaesser, "Myth as the Phantasmagoria of History: H.-J. Syberberg,

The pages that follow are not a historical study but an essay, or, more exactly, the bringing together of two essays that could be taken separately. The first consists of chapters 1, 2, and 4; it represents the main part of the text, a study of the basic elements of the new discourse, as well as of some of the earlier modes of fascination with kitsch and death. The second essay, limited to chapter 3, aims at clarifying some of the ways in which the criminal side of Nazism is neutralized in the contemporary mind by artifices of language, displacements of meaning, aesthetization, inversion of symbols. These two essays are obviously two facets of the same problem: The more the worst aspects of Nazism are neutralized, the more the new discourse finds its way into our imagination.

Finally, a warning to the reader is necessary. The following pages are designed to advance understanding of a phenomenon that has escaped us. Since I cannot mostly have recourse to rigorous proof, I shall utilize several angles of approach, and sometimes, whenever abstract exposition could only fail, I shall directly evoke the styles or atmospheres of the works discussed.

Indeed, this type of "re-presentation" will be frequent in the first two chapters in order to provide our analysis with basic materials and a necessary point of departure.

Cinema and Representation," *New German Critique* 24–25, Fall–Winter 1981–82. As already mentioned, there is no necessary link between the level of the images and the other levels.

1

Every frisson is a response to surprise, to an unexpected comparison or the revelation of a hitherto unnoticed reality. Here, it is the meeting of kitsch and death.

Kitsch, that "pinnacle of good taste in the absence of taste, of art in ugliness—a branch of mistletoe under the lamp in a railway waiting room, nickeled plate glass in a public place, artificial flowers gone astray in Whitechapel, a lunch box decorated with Vosges fir—everyday *Gemütlichkeit,* art adapted to life where the function of the adaptation exceeds that of innovation. All this is kitsch, the hidden, tender, and sweet vice—and who can live without vices? And that is where its insinuating power and universality begin. . . ."[1]

It should be stressed at the outset that I shall be dealing only with some limited aspects of kitsch, those directly relevant to the purpose of this essay. Kitsch is adapted to the tastes of the majority, a faithful expression of a common sensibility, of the harmony dear to the petit bourgeois, who see in it a respect for beauty and for the order of things—for the established order and for things as they are.

It is the juxtaposition of the kitsch aesthetic and of the themes of death that creates the surprise, that special frisson so characteristic not only of the new discourse but also, it appears, of Nazism itself.

Is it necessary to see in this the will to reconstitute an atmosphere or a fascination? Both, no doubt. Beneath today's reflection, one catches a glimpse of certain fundamental components of yesterday's Nazi hold on the imagination.

There is a kitsch of death. For example, death transformed into sweet sleep: the "good night, sweet prince" of the last scene of *Hamlet,* the conventions of the American funeral parlor, or the death of the patriarch in morally uplifting books. The death of heroes, too: He collapses, his eyes already dulled, one hand at the wound where blood spills, but the other still gripping the broken flagstaff; any child in a school yard who mimics the death of a cowboy or Indian, cop or thief, Mafioso or incorruptible gives a kitsch performance of death. There is even a kitsch of the apocalypse: the livid sky slashed by immense purple reflections, flames surging from cities, flocks and men fleeing toward the glowing horizon, and far, very far away, four horsemen. And yet this kitsch of death, of destruction, of apocalypse is a special kitsch, a representation of reality that does not integrate into the vision of ordinary kitsch.

In ordinary kitsch there is an equivalence between the representation of reality and what could exist in reality: Lovers actually do lie under a fir tree like two turtledoves; a cottage from whose chimney a thin tendril of smoke rises could indeed harbor a happy family; a Swiss landscape does resemble a picture postcard. But faced with a kitsch representation of death, everyone knows that here two contradictory elements are amalgamated: on the one hand, an appeal to harmony, to emotional communion at the simplest and most immediate level; on the other, solitude and terror. It has often been said that one of the characteristics of kitsch is precisely the neutralization of "extreme situations," particularly death, by turning them into some sentimental idyll.* This is undoubtedly true at the level of kitsch production, hardly so at the level of individual experience, when one has to imagine or to face death. As I have just mentioned, whatever the kitsch images surrounding one, death creates an *authentic* feeling of loneliness and dread. Basically, at the level of individual experience, kitsch and death remain incompatible. The juxtaposition of these two contradictory elements represents the foundation of a certain religious aesthetic, and, in my opinion, the bedrock of Nazi aesthetics as well as the new evocation of Nazism. Here for example is the description of the night of August 23, 1939, in Speer's memoirs:

> In the course of the night we stood on the terrace of the Berghof with Hitler and marveled at a rare natural spectacle. Northern lights of unusual intensity threw red light on the legend-haunted Untersberg across the valley,

*See for instance Ludwig Giesz, *Phänomenologie des Kitsches* (Munich: Wilhelm Fink Verlag, 1971), p. 39.

while the sky above shimmered in all the colors of the rainbow. The last act of *Götterdämmerung* could not have been more effectively staged. The same red light bathed our faces and our hands. The display produced a curiously pensive mood among us. Abruptly turning to one of his military adjutants, Hitler said: "Looks like a great deal of blood. This time we won't bring it off without violence."[2]

This is kitsch brought to perfection; someone on his way to becoming the most powerful man in the world (the pact just signed with the Soviet Union constitutes an enormous leap forward) stands in his aerie surrounded by a spectacular mountain landscape. (It should be noted in passing that when he sensed defeat approaching, Hitler burrowed into his bunker beneath the Reich Chancellery. Here we have a fascinating adaptation of habitat to the parabola of a career.) Hitler's face is turned toward a night sky slashed by strange red lights, the color of blood. This is the poet facing a storm-swept lake, an assassin fleeing under a purple sky, zebra-striped by lights. Moreover, the author adds the Untersberg tableau, so haunted by legends. (The emperor Frederick Barbarossa is said to sleep in the mountains of the Harz, Charlemagne in the Untersberg.) Then suddenly Hitler turns to one of his military aides and says, "Looks like a great deal of blood. This time we won't bring it off without violence." It is the announcement of destruction and death—not only in the scene described but in the retrospective imagination of the reader.

After the grandiose fresco, the colored lithograph with gilded garlands and colored glass beads. The menacing and somber point is there, but camouflaged and in a corner in back. This is the vision the collaborator Robert Brasillach had of fascism (and fascism obviously includes Nazism here), a vision at least as Jacques Laurent has reconstructed it: the glass beads, the tinsel, the fake jewels, the galleys launched on the Mare Nostrum, Hitler celebrating the Walpurgis nights, the garlands of marching songs and forget-me-nots, the fir branches, the gathered huckleberries on blond plaits, the archangel Michael's legion, the SS come down from the Venusberg amid the somber foliage, Spanish olive trees waving in the wind ready to become laurel wreaths, the oak of Saint Louis—and the final fettering "trembling with the same movement as the oak of Saint Louis, the cedar of the crusades and the waves of the Atlantic engulfing Mermoz."[3]

Ancient legends and bucolic countrysides. And, suddenly, the blow of destiny, brief, without appeal: "the waves of the Atlantic engulfing Mermoz." The kitsch was there. Death could not be far off.

It has been said that fascism was a revolt against modernity, the result of the crisis of a society passing from a traditional framework to that of industrialism, a rebellion designed to create a deliberately archaic utopia. A glance at our colored lithograph confirms this aspect of fascism, and of Nazism in particular; no cities in the space where heroes move, no factories, no combines, large dams or electrification. This is far from the Soviet ideal, where the iconography of singing tomorrows avoids themes of death and destruction. We are faced with the mysterious and virginal nature of the countries of legends, and the hero is broken to bits as he enters the modern era: "the waves of the Atlantic engulfing Mermoz."

The kitsch here is a return to a debased romantic inspiration, to an aesthetic stripped of the force and novelty it had 150 years ago at the dawn of modernity.* And it is in this pre- and antimodern ambience that the opposing themes of harmonious kitsch and death flower and spread. A major theme thrown up by the multiple reflections of this juxtaposition is that of the hero. The hero being, to be sure, he who will die.

This is not the Hans Castorp of *The Magic Mountain,* though he will disappear in the maelstrom of World War I, but rather his cousin Joachim. It is the Conrad of Marguerite Yourcenar's prewar classic tale *Coup de Grâce:*

> Conrad did not even know the meaning of the word [fear]. There are such beings, often the most fragile of all, who live at ease with death, as if in their native element. One often hears of this special gift, almost an investiture, in consumptive patients destined to die young, but I have sometimes seen youths who were headed for violent death manifesting that same lightness of heart which is both their essential virtue and their privilege as young gods. . . .[4]

*"To a large extent we can see kitsch as a hackneyed form of romanticism," writes Matei Calinescu in his *Faces of Modernity: Avant-Garde, Decadence, Kitsch* ([Bloomington: Indiana University Press, 1977], p. 240). He quotes Hermann Broch's essay "Notes on the Problem of Kitsch," which establishes the same link between kitsch and romanticism, basing his parallel on their common nostalgic quality. *Ibid,* see infra my own reference to Nazism as nostalgia. The paradox of kitsch and modernity is that kitsch is often an antimodern face of modernity. For a general presentation of the kitsch element in Nazi imagination and in its German foundations, see also Herman Glaser, *The Cultural Roots of National Socialism* (Austin: University of Texas Press, 1978).

They are the heroes in Ernst von Salomon's *The Out-laws* or the fighters in Ernst Jünger's *Storm of Steel,* and, as well, their epigones. Here we are in Kalten-born's SS prytaneum, which Michel Tournier evokes in *The Ogre.* It is the last year of the war and the *Jüngmannen* celebrate the summer solstice:

> The smallest boy came forward and walked toward the pyre. In his hand he carried a little point of fire, quivering and light as a butterfly. . . . He jumped back as the flame leaped up with a roar. The clear voices rose in the flickering darkness. . . . The fire of other columns could be seen in the distance. . . . The Jüngmannen filed around in a circle, and each in turn sprang forward and leaped through the flames. . . . This time there is no need for interpretation or for any deciphering grid. This ceremony, obstinately mingling the future and death, and throwing the boys one after the other into the live coals, is the clear evocation, the diabolic invocation, of the massacre of the innocent toward which we march singing.
>
> I'd be surprised if Kaltenborn had the chance to celebrate another summer solstice.[5]

In another register, this one autobiographical, but with the same basic theme, the rite of passage, of initiation, Christian de La Mazière speaks of his first Hitler salute at the moment of joining the Waffen SS, also during the last year of the war:

"I was proud of the Hitler salute because it struck me as signifying a new start, and through it I was entering an order of things where nothing was easy but where all was more pure and honest."[6] And then, later on, he says

31

of his last meeting with La Buharaye, his comrade in battle, "This was the last sight I had of my friend, of my big brother. He disappeared, and must have been killed. He had entered my life with a smile; his cold blue Viking eyes; the unlucky Breton, he went out with another smile. . . ."[7]

In Tournier, as in La Mazière, the young heroes belong to the elite, to the SS: pupils at an SS prytaneum, German Waffen SS and French volunteers. In both cases they are young and pure, in both cases destined to die.

The theme of purity hauntingly returns through a whole series of symbols: the extreme youth of the *Jungmannen,* which evokes the massacre of the innocents, the fire, the spark, an order "where everything was purer," blue eyes and La Buharaye's smile.* This is a key theme, a carrier of all the sentimentality in an enormous literature of uplift and edification; here it provides a striking contrast to the cruelty and injustice of a destiny that has decreed death. It also brings together all the themes underlying a certain kind of religiosity and antimodernism: God calls home to Him all the entirely pure beings, who are much too pure in some ways to stay long on this earth. It is the traditional image of the lives of the saints, the central axis of a whole religious education: "purity" as an absolute criterion of value. Thus the myth of the hero, along with its ethical and aesthetic baggage, relies on the diffuse and insinuating imagery of the Christian religious tradition, which gives its evocations their emotional power.

*In *The Captive Dreamer,* La Mazière writes also of "these beings without defect or flaw who would never rot or decay."

Another recurring theme is that of ancient cults (the ceremony of the summer solstice in Tournier's novel), of the lands of legends ("Viking," "the hard luck Breton"). Archaism was one of the striking characteristics of the group to which La Mazière, La Buharaye, and their friends belonged.

Finally, there is the archetype, as represented by Conrad in *Coup de Grâce.* (Note again the obsession with purity faced with putrefaction.)

Natures like Conrad's are frail and feel their best when clad in armor. Turned loose in the world of society or of business, lionized by women or prey to easy success, they are subject to certain insidious dissolution, like the loathsome decay of iris; those sombre flowers, though nobly shaped like a lance, die miserably in their own sticky secretion, in marked contrast to the slow, heroic dying of the rose.[8]

Conrad is the knight opposed to a world of women and of business, the pure soul facing a world enfeebled and decayed by modernity.

And thus the young hero destined for death is surrounded by a nimbus of complex emotions; he is the carrier of either one of two banners, one proclaiming an implicit religious tradition, the other that of a cult of primitive and archaic values. He confronts that which denies them: the abject world of modernity, the obscure weight of material powers, the revolting inanity of nonhuman factors.* Unvanquished unto death, the

*This is very much how, in his own way, Michel Tournier speaks of the German soldiers: "We knew that no army in the world had the force to resist

hero takes on an almost supernatural incandescence.

These men, therefore, belong to a religious order, in a literal and figurative sense, to a secret elite united for a confrontation of civilizations. Here once again Christian de La Mazière on his entry into the Waffen SS:

This arm extended, I was at once proud and embarrassed. It seemed to me that I had passed a threshold, and that in passing it, I was dimly dismissing something from where I had come: my land, my past, the traditions of my country. But these men fascinated me and I wanted to incorporate myself there. I perceived them as strong, generous and pitiless: beings without weakness who would never putrefy.[9]

In each of these evocations of the Nazi's French soldiers of the Charlemagne division, of the Waffen SS in general, of the whole aspect of collaboration,* still another quality tirelessly reappears, that of fidelity. Thus the last French Waffen SS are going to die "when the day comes in one of the two places where Adolf Hitler has decided to die among his most faithful soldiers: the Prussian capital or the Bavarian redoubt."†

The profile of the hero dedicated to sacrifice becomes clear: He is a pure being, haloed by religiosity, rooted in the world of timeless values, faithful unto death. This

---

it and that everything depended on the amount of land one would hold to pitch camp. France resisted for three weeks. England would have been occupied in fifteen days. The USA would have held out for two months. As for the Soviets, they had only been saved by the infinity, aggravated by winter, they had behind them. . . ." (*Le Vent Paraclet* [Paris: Gallimard, 1977], p. 73.)

*See Jean Mabire in *La Division Charlemagne: Les combats des SS français en Poméranie* (Paris: Fayard, 1974).

†Ibid., p. 586.

whole arsenal is reminiscent of the moralizing literature of religious schools and the Boy Scouts: Guy de Larigaudie and his companions are eternal adolescents. It is Brasillach's "deep morning," "the last faithful soldiers" of the Charlemagne division, and a thousand and one other models drawn from the Nazi imagination itself.

Take, for example, a classic of its kind, *Hitler Junge Quex (Hitler Youth Quex)*, one of the most famous films of the early days of the Nazi regime. Everything is there: Young Herbert Norkus leaves behind the dissolute Reds —who drink, smoke, consort with girls, and sing raucous songs—in order to partake of the purity that surrounds the young Hitlerians with their campfires, their sunrise rituals, their bathing in clear streams. Norkus, the pure young hero, will die for a cause to which, henceforth, he consecrates his strength and—killed in 1932 by the Communists—his life.[10]

Again and again, new associations form around this juxtaposition of kitsch and death, new emotional layers appear, and one begins to have some notion of the resonances of the new discourse. (One notes that it deploys diverse modes of expression: first-rate historical reminiscence [Albert Speer], pop history [Jean Mabire], literature that aims at a large audience [Christian de La Mazière], a novel both readable and demanding that can be taken at the most varied levels [Michel Tournier], a masterpiece of the experimental cinema that has become one of the most "in" films of recent years [Hans-Jürgen Syberberg].)

In the published text of Syberberg's *Hitler, a Film from Germany*, a scene appears that was not filmed: While the audience hears the roll of memorial drums for the dead of the failed Nazi coup of November 9, 1923, two faithful SS men search desperately for their lost Führer. In a march that will never end, they walk arm in arm along the roads of the Obersalzberg, then push into a tunnel leading to Hitler's teahouse. Syberberg writes,

we hear the text of Heine's ballad about two [of Napoleon's] grenadiers . . . waiting for the resurrection of their leader from the grave. The ballad ends with a "Marseillaise" as composed by Richard Wagner. A daring, terrifying vision. Two laughing lemurs of the netherworld—the eternal Nazi wandering across the world, like a primal image, in the drumming collapse of his continuous and expected resurrection.[11]

The juxtaposition of kitsch and death is done here on two simultaneously different levels of expression. In the background, perhaps the best-known and most often quoted ballad in German poetry (Heine's "The Two Grenadiers"); it is, to be sure, the comforting call of popular culture. And at the same time the two heroes, dead and alive at once, marching toward eternity.

Directly related to the sequence not filmed, but more important, is the sequence Syberberg devotes to the monologue of Hitler's valet, K. W. Krause. The valet describes, with minute attention to the least detail, how Hitler dressed himself, and what his daily habits were ("Hitler changed his underwear as he needed to . . . up to three times a day, and then not at all for two or three days. He wore only the thinnest socks, even in his boots"). And simultaneously, either superimposed or alternating with Krause's description, a radio documen-

tary begins: the Christmas Eve 1942 broadcast of the
Wehrmacht radio: "I am again calling . . . the Bay of
Biscay . . . Leningrad . . . the Caucasus front, the U-boat
sailors in the Atlantic. . . ." And the stations identified
themselves and replied. . . .

Meanwhile, Krause continues his story (on the
screen, snow starts falling):

On Christmas Eve of the year 1937, Hitler greatly aston-
ished me. He was in his private apartment in Munich,
at number 16 Prinzregentenplatz. I myself was invited
to a family gathering, and I was greatly looking forward to the moment when Hitler would withdraw and
I would thus be free to leave. But then he walked
through the room containing some presents that had
not yet been distributed, he wanted to pick out one more
gift.

The two of us then wrapped it up, as we stretched out
on the carpet, and . . . as he pressed down upon the knot,
I tied up his thumb as a joke, whereupon, laughing, he
gave me a playful blow on the back of my neck. . . .

While the Wehrmacht station establishes contact
with all the battlefronts, from the northern cape to
Tunis, and from the Atlantic to the Caucasus, Krause
tells how Hitler dragged him along on a crazy tour of
Munich in a taxi that Christmas Eve, constantly changing the instructions he gave the driver, until they finally
got out in front of the Café Luitpold. And during this
time on the Wehrmacht station:

We ask you, comrades, to sing once more the lovely old
Christmas carol "Silent Night." . . .
All stations will now join us with this spontaneous

greeting by comrades deep in the south, on the Black Sea.

Now they are already singing in the Arctic Ocean off Finland, and now we are switching in all the other stations, Leningrad, Stalingrad.

And now France . . . Catane . . . Africa.

And now they are all singing together:

. . . Sleep in heavenly peace. . . .

Hitler and Krause do not go into the café, but walk back, still unrecognized, toward the Königliche Platz: "And so, recognized by no one, we managed to get back to our place on the Prinzregentenstrasse. . . ."

Documentary. Call to the dead of November 9, 1923.

Documentary. Announcement from Radio Belgrade: "This is the Wehrmacht station Lili Marleen. We greet our listeners!"

En route, we were overtaken by an icy rain, so that, after having previously only leaned on my shoulder, he went the rest of the way arm in arm with me, since he was wearing new patent-leather shoes. Yes, someone must have noticed something. For the next day, Himmler and Rattenhüber, who was in charge of the escort detachment of the criminal investigation department, reproached me for not telling anyone in advance about this undertaking.[12]

No matter what their actual age, this is the world of boys, with its pranks (the master, incognito, out at night with his valet) but also its nostalgia and above all the loyalty of a juvenile fraternity to its own norms, to the one among them who becomes the chief (the two ex–SS men, the two grenadiers). Hitler remained an eternal adolescent: gauche, sprung from modest circumstances, never at ease in his polished shoes; oh, so simple with Krause—his valet, to be sure, but above all a companion, with whom he squats on the rug, whom he slaps on the back, with whom he can laugh loudly. And, on a second level, in counterpoint, the fraternity of young heroes who are going to die: "Comrades, we ask you one more time to sing the beautiful old Christmas carol . . ." Not "Deutschland, Deutschland über alles," not "Heute gehört uns Deutschland," not the "Horst Wessel Lied," but the song of nostalgia, of home, of piety: "Silent Night, Holy Night." The universe of purity fuses with that of religious imagery, with the mythic candor that marks the beginnings of the world.

Kitsch emotion represents a certain kind of simplified, degraded, insipid, but all the more insinuating romanticism. All of us live among kitsch; we are plunged into it up to our necks. Hence the importance and the hold this type of imagery and sentiment has on us, a hold that is formed into frisson thanks to the counterpoint of death and destruction. Thus in Syberberg's film the ballad of the two grenadiers, the phantomlike nostalgia of the two ex–SS men, the radio hookup among the stations of the global battlefield, the systematic utilization of rolling funeral drums, and the call to the dead of November 9, 1923. Death *and* nostalgia, for the latter is particularly powerful in fascism in general and in Nazism in particular. By definition, for Nazism looks backward, back to the lost premodern world, the archaic universe of before the deluge. Unlike Marxism, which reaches out to the society of tomorrow whose advent is assured and which will be totally different. Liberalism, too, turns toward the future—harmoniously or not, mankind will progress under the sign of evolution and of rationality. For Nazism, however, the model of future society is only a reflection of the past.

Syberberg's juxtaposition of these themes is intentional, but no matter what work is chosen, the same structure reappears. In Rainer Werner Fassbinder's *Lili Marleen,* the director quotes Goebbels as saying, "A melodramatic song on top of a macabre dance." This is not only the film's theme, apropos of the celebrated song; it is as well a statement of the aesthetic of the Third Reich and the aesthetic of its reflection in a certain kind of imagery. Here, in fact, it is no longer a matter of the juxtaposition of kitsch and death but their perfect synthesis. Kitsch death is a means to digest the past. The bluish tinge of the war scenes, the pensive soldiers in their trenches, and, suddenly, at the end of the three minutes of grace provided by the song, hell surging up again, with red and ochre flames, and always the same corpse shown projected with the same movement into the air, the same tank with the cannon on its turret directed toward the same house collapsing under the shelling. Then again bluish light, silence, and the song . . .

A kitsch of death with symbolic subtleties. For death appears in diverse forms in this film, like the definitive German apocalypse, which is present in filigree. One sees the prefiguration in the scene on the bridge, when the Jew with a killer's head, taking no notice of orders received, breaks the universal code of honor (one does not kill a representative of the enemy come to negotiate) and blows up the whole Nazi delegation in a sudden, powerful explosion. But this, too, raises some of the maneuvers of the exorcism, of a certain way of representing the Jews by inverting the symbols. I will return to this.

One couldn't insist too much on the primordial aspect of the theme of death in Nazism itself, although that has often been shown elsewhere. Thus in a 1975 article devoted to Leni Riefensthal's book of photographs, *The Last of the Nuba,* Susan Sontag shows how yet again the most famous of the Third Reich's filmmakers returns to a favorite theme: "[Riefensthal] seems right on target with her choice, as a photographic subject, of a society whose most enthusiastic and lavish ceremony is the funeral. *Viva la muerta!*"[13]

A comment by the Germanist J. P. Stern on Syberberg's *Hitler, a Film from Germany* underlines this same obsession. Beyond economic or political objectives, what formed the basis of the Nazi world view, what drove Hitler and his acolytes, "was the fascination that destruction and the love of death exercised on them."[14]

Finally, in his biography of Hitler, Joachim Fest shows how Hitler's talents as a "director" were truly deployed only during funeral ceremonies:

Life seemed to paralyze his inspiration. . . . On the other hand his pessimistic temperament tirelessly won new lighting effects from the ceremony of death. The carefully developed artistic demagoguery had real high points, when he strode down the broad avenue between hundreds of thousands to honor the dead on the Königs-platz in Munich or on the grounds of the Nürnberg party congress with gloomy music in the background, for example. In such scenes out of a political Good Friday magic—"magnificence is used to advertise death," as Adorno said about Wagner's music—Hitler's idea of aesthetic politics matches the concept.

He also had a distinct preference for nocturnal back-drops. Torches, pyres, or flaming wheels were continu-ally being kindled. Though such rituals were supposed to be highly positive and inspirational, in fact they struck another note, stirring apocalyptic associations and awakening a fear of universal conflagration or doom, including each individual's own.[15]

This carries all the weight of a romantic tradition, particularly the German, nourished on the theme of death. There is also the whole influence of twentieth-century German literature: Rilke, George, Mann; of the expressionists and of the German cinema of the Twen-ties—an art rejected by the Nazis, who nevertheless participated in the sensibility behind it and who of course adopted and integrated its themes. In short, one breathes again the air breathed in Germany before and, especially, after World War I. And, above all, Wagner and always Wagner. For the Nazis, this motif of death takes on a special dimension—urgent, essential, in some ways religious, mythical. This is an attraction for death in itself, as something elemental, opaque, intract-able to analysis. The new discourse takes up these themes again and faithfully transposes them.

Thus Visconti's film *The Damned* is a work totally turned toward death—physically and symbolically: the assassination of the patriarch Joachim von Essenbeck; the murder of Elisabeth Thalmann and her granddaughter in a camp; the suicide of the little Jewish girl, Lisa; the massacre of the SA leadership during "the night of the long knives"; finally the marriage-suicide of Sophie von Essenbeck and her lover, Friedrich Bruckmann. On a symbolic level, all these events converge to suggest the decline and decay of a world seized by a rising Hitlerism, from the insistent evocation of the decomposition of an industrial empire and of a family, to indirect artistic and literary references—to Wagner, Schopenhauer, and above all to Thomas Mann, the Mann of *Buddenbrooks, Death in Venice, Mario and the Magician,* and *The Magic Mountain*—and finally down to the apocalyptic details, such as the first and last glimmer of the blast furnaces.

Thematic analysis, however, is not what counts. The important thing is the constant identification of Nazism and death; not real death in its everyday horror and tragic banality, but a ritualized, stylized, and aestheticized death, a death that wills itself the carrier of horror, decrepitude, and monstrosity, but which ultimately and definitely appears as a poisonous apotheosis.

The two big scenes of *The Damned* are the SA massacre and the marriage-suicide of Sophie and Friedrich. In the one, death is a final explosion, like an orgiastic paroxysm, following a furious sexual debauch, a dazzling pagan feast. The other is a ceremonial parody, where two cyanide capsules represent a gift to the nuptial couple, but a parody with magnificent colors and Nazi uniforms, with ritual grandeur and Hitler salutes at the end, with an allusion to Macbeth and Lady Macbeth, or to Tristan and Isolde joined in eternal damnation. In Visconti's film, as in so many others, Nazi death is a show, a production, a performance. For the viewer, everything signifies fascination, terror, and ecstasy.

But this fascination with death only reaches full intensity when death appears as a "revelation." The religious roots of this vision of death are evident, with this exception: In the Christian religious tradition, death signifies the revelation of an elsewhere at once mysterious and concrete, vague yet certain. There is none of that in Nazi death. One of the final scenes of Tournier's novel *The Ogre* makes the case:

> The flagstones of the terrace were covered by a carpet of spotless snow untouched by the thaw. The balustrade was also white, save at the foot of the three swords, where it was stained red, as if a crimson mantle had been thrown under each. All three of them were there, Hajo, Haro and Lothar, the red-haired twins, faithfully flanking their friend, the boy with white hair—pierced from omega to alpha, their eyes staring into space, the three swords making in each a different wound. . . . The stars had gone out, and the Golgotha of boys stood out against a black sky.[16]

Kitsch and frightfulness are created here by the accumulation of images of terror and death and by the symbols of a pseudospirituality: the swords, the night, the three impaled victims, the bloodstains on the immaculate snow, eyes wide open staring into space, the stars extinguished, Golgotha, the black sky, etc. We are at the very heart of the aesthetic dimension of the new discourse on Nazism. Here is the essence of the frisson: an overload of symbols; a baroque setting; an evocation of a mysterious atmosphere, of the myth and of religiosity enveloping a vision of death announced as a revelation opening out into nothing—nothing but frightfulness and the night. Unless . . . Unless the revelation is that of a mysterious force leading man toward irresistible destruction.

In *The Three Faces of Fascism,* Ernst Nolte claims that as opposed to traditional religious visions and, in other respects, to Marxism and liberalism, fascism is a "refusal of transcendence." Too vaguely phrased to allow scientific debate, this is interesting only as a metaphor for an ambiguous reality. Looking at it more closely, however, one can perceive the notion of a kind of negative transcendence: Man and his world are dominated by a blind destiny that leads to inevitable destruction.

That is why the theme of the hero appears with such insistence, endowed with a new dimension: The hero is the one who remains faithful to his destiny despite his lucid perception of destruction and of death. But here Nazism brings in "the community of the saints": The dead continue to march with the living toward an inexorable destiny (*"marschieren im Geist in unseren Reihen mit"*—"march in spirit in our ranks"). The commemoration of the dead of November 9 expresses this central element of the Nazi liturgy, along with the "Horst Wessel Lied," the theme of the eternal watch *(die ewige Wache)*. In the last scene of the 1933 film *Hans Westmar* (a stylized history of party hero Horst Wessel, an

SA man killed by Communists, at least according to official propaganda), the murdered hero's funeral begins in a menacing atmosphere. The cortege, poorly protected by police, is surrounded by a hostile crowd. The mob breaks through the barriers and runs wild. The burial of the dead man nevertheless takes place in the presence of his companions, and then, while the music swells, Hans Westmar himself appears, a flag in his fist, superimposed on a background of storm clouds. And here is the sublime vision: The SA marches to the strains of the "Horst Wessel Lied" and Hans Westmar marches in step with his comrades.[17]

It is a long way from this apotheosis of the regime's early years to the later funeral ceremonies, notably after the fall of Stalingrad. And it is a long way from the glorious marches of the SA (with their dreams of the ultimate revolution) to the somber communion with the dead of the SS. And it is precisely this "somber communion" that the new discourse takes up again.

And so we return to the pseudo-spirituality that envelops such kitsch, finding there constant exploitations of esotericism and mystery as well as the no less frequent evocation of the universe of legends and myths.*

"Myth," Michel Tournier writes in *Le Vent Paraclet*,[18] "is basic history. . . . It is a history everyone already knows." He himself has built a lacework of myths in *The Ogre*. Intuitively or consciously, the creators of the new discourse on Nazism feel that this is fertile soil, a

---

*For a description of the intimate link between myth and kitsch, or legend and kitsch, see Gillo Dorfles, "Myth and Kitsch," in *Kitsch: The World of Bad Taste* (New York: 1969), pp. 46ff; Walther Killy, *Deutscher Kitsch* (Göttingen: 1961), pp. 27ff.

terrain on which to hunt, a gleam that must be seized once again.

In effect, every approach to mythic narrative not tied to formal structure alone but leaning toward narrative content as the carrier of real significance—as in the work of Jung, Eliade, Barthes, Tournier—shows that through often insignificant, conjectural, or pedestrian narration, myth transmits (for the ideological purpose of asserting the power of the ruling class, Barthes would say; for the purpose of authentic disclosure, enhancing the primordial and the sacred, as Jung, Eliade, and Tournier would say) a message that strives for universal significance. Again, take the most banal of our stories, *Lili Marleen.*

The true story of Lale Anderson and her song is a small event in the midst of a world conflict. Nevertheless, there is a mythic character in the meteoric rise of a small-time singer whose sentimental refrain is sung by millions on both sides, the nostalgia amid the din of bombs and the thunder of cannon. The communicating principle here is the elemental power of emotion, nostalgia, and love, all stronger than hatred and death. But for whom?

This is where Fassbinder adds one more important level to the initial structure of the myth. For ordinary people, he tells us, the simple soldiers of all nations, for the people to whom the film's singer belongs. Arrayed against these fundamentally good, generous, courageous people (one need only look at the faces of the soldiers), arranged against these millions of anonymous heroes who are going to be sacrificed (six million, Fassbinder tells us) are the powers of evil, those who hold the power and the money: Jewish capitalists on the one hand, embodied by the patriarch of Zürich; Nazism on the other, symbolized by this vivid light, Adolf Hitler. And thus the real struggle is not between the Nazis and their enemies, but between the forces of evil (Jewish capitalism and Nazism) on the one hand, and the good people (Wickie and her song, that devil of a good pianist, and the millions of anonymous soldiers) on the other: those who are going to die.

The story also has its hidden hero, hiding behind the mask of evil to serve the good: Hinkel's adjutant, who, in an SS uniform, helps the resistance. It has, as well, a specious hero, the young Jew Robert Mendelsohn, a contemptible fellow, a coward and a traitor—though at first he appears to be a good human being. At the beginning he is shown as taking the peoples' side and opposed to the patriarch, as someone who has proved his courage and is capable of love. But he returns to the clan and is linked forever to power, money, glory. At the end of the film, it is he, the adored orchestra conductor, who will embody the triumph of Jewish capitalism while Wickie is thrown out into darkness.

In the final reckoning, where will victory go in the real battle being waged behind the apparent one? Wickie has been abandoned and capitalism seems the great victor. But just before this last scene it is Hinkel's aide, the unknown resistance fighter, who has the ultimate word. He explains to Wickie that they will probably have to wait a long time before being rehabilitated, but the hope remains: Their battle will be recognized. No doubt Wickie and her companion, too, will see the light at the end of the tunnel, and, symbolically, together with them, the good will perhaps emerge into full day.

Myth, in its function as a revealer of truths and basic and hidden values, is the source of power and inspiration, the vehicle of coherence, the harbinger of an enduring present. In the introduction to the text of his film, Syberberg has clearly seen the almost necessary relationship, in the Nazi era as well as today, between myth and kitsch: "The key to modern myths is in the banality (taken seriously) of kitsch success and the popularity of triviality—final traces of worlds gone under."[19] Kitsch is a debased form of myth, but nevertheless draws from the mythic substance—a part of its emotional impact—the death of the hero; the eternal march, the twilight of the gods; myth is a footprint, an echo of lost worlds, haunting an imagination invaded by excessive rationality and thus becoming the crystallization point for thrusts of the archaic and of the irrational.

In *Lili Marleen,* everything is kitsch and at the same time everything breathes uplift and edification. Despite appearances, there is little irony in the film. Everything in it has the rhythm of legend, of the sacred. Good and evil are recognized. Beneath the melodramatic aspect of the story (a sweet, loving, poor girl is abandoned by a rich young man), one sees the mark of the great tragedies. It is also the mythic annulment of time that reveals to us that the story recounted here is not a simple episode but the expression of eternal verities represented by stereotypes rather than by specific characters. As if to verify this observation, there is no change throughout the film in the faces or demeanor of the characters, who are seen for the first time in 1938 and for the last in 1945. In seven years—and what years for each of them!—they do not add one wrinkle or show the least trace of aging. They are outside time.

Thus in the aesthetics of the new discourse, as, without doubt, in Nazism itself, it is a matter of the juxtaposition of opposing images of harmony (kitsch) and death, and of such violently contradictory feelings as harmony and terror. But this double series of images and of content is carried by a specific language, whether in films or in books. This language, because of its formal aspect and its external characteristics, plays a role in the aesthetic hold on the imagination I have tried to put in evidence in the course of this chapter, just as it will have its function, as we shall see, in the "Hitler effect," and its decisive place in the maneuvers of exorcism.

A first glance reveals that this language is one of accumulation, repetition, and redundancy: a massive use of synonyms, an excess of similar epithets, a play of images sent back, in turn, from one to the other in echoes without end. This is not the linear language of interconnected argument nor of step-by-step demonstration; this is, under a less immediate but no less systematic and no less effective form, the circular language of invocation, which tirelessly turns on itself and creates a kind of hypnosis by repetition, like a word that is chanted in certain prayers, a dance that persists in the same rhythm unto frenzy, a call of the tom-tom, or, quite simply, the heavy music of our parades, the muffled stomping of marching legions. The roll of drums and the call to the dead during the commemoration of November 9, 1923, which punctuates Syberberg's film, as well as the incessant repetition of certain Nazi songs in the background, are deliberate cinematographic expressions of this kind of language pushed to the extreme. In *Lili Marleen* it is clearly the repetition of the song as leitmotiv that creates a similar effect, as does the reprise of the same scenes in a stylized manner, the flamboyant setting of Berlin's Sportpalast, with its thousands of soldiers and the repeated shots of swastika banners. . . .

Less obvious but perhaps no less effective is the constant play of synonyms, the repetition of similar images, which nourishes and reinforces a display and an emotion central to the purpose. Take as an example the following excerpt from a spoken chorus in commemoration of November 9:

We are building the eternal Feldherrnhallen of the Reich, the marches which lead into eternity until the hammers fall out of our hands. Then let us wall ourselves into the breast of these altars. . . .*

One immediately perceives the repetition of the word *eternal* or *eternity,* but all the other images in this text in fact express the same thing. The Feldherrnhalle is the mausoleum honoring (for eternity) the great chieftains of war, hammers fall from the hands of those entering upon eternal sleep. Here eternal sleep is also eternal communion, as the prayer rises to heaven: Let us wall ourselves inside the breast of these altars, etc.

Thus the structure of the language and the form of the

*Cited in Klaus Vondung, *Magie und Manipulation, Ideologischer Kult und politische Religion des Nationalsozialismus* (Göttingen: Vondenhoeck & Ruprecht, 1971), p. 38.

discourse support the religious and mythical content of the proposed images. And the rhythmic repetition adds to the incantatory effect.

It would be useless, it seems to me, to return here to the texts of the new discourse in order to discover more accumulations of similar examples. Each of the texts cited contains ample proof. The theme of death, for example, is taken up again from every possible angle, and everywhere one can find the linkage of the images of night, of fire, of the long march without end, etc. But that brings back, whether it is a matter of Nazism or its reflection, one aspect of the problem that remains difficult to explain: the result these proceedings engendered. One knows how the sight of ten thousand banners rising all at once overcame the spectators at Nürnberg, how the serried ranks of a hundred thousand men massed on the meeting grounds overwhelmed them—though in incomprehensible ways. In an attenuated form, it is the same for the type of language we are examining.

Indeed, the accumulation of which I speak can and does evoke two opposing reactions: The elimination of all free space, the proliferation even of images, can create in the spectator or the reader an impression of fusion and of sugary harmony that reflects kitsch in general and, more particularly, those feelings of communion and of vague religiosity that suffuse Nazism and its reflections.* But the same accumulation, the same

---

*Cumulation is a characteristic of kitsch: "The word," writes Walther Killy, "gets the emotional prop from the adjective or the attribute. The theme so created is bolstered by similar themes and linked to them: an 'atmosphere' just created needs to be maintained, its fleeting and superficial character needs permanence and interiorization. That is why motive becomes linked to motive, as the word and its epithet were already linked. The uncertainty of the author about the aim of his text brought about one of the most frequent characteristics of literary kitsch: cumulation." (Killy, *Deutscher Kitsch*, p. 14.)

serried rhythm of repeated images, of sounds, of similar terms, also suggests drowning, suffocation, terror, and chaos. Thus the dichotomy of themes we have put in evidence is mirrored back in the contradictory aspects of language in order to create the particular effect for which it will be necessary, in terms of this essay, to offer an explanation.

2

"On July 31 [1815]," Jean Tulard writes in his book on Napoleon, "Lord Keith went on board the *Bellérophon* to tell the emperor that he would be deported to Saint Helena. Napoleon's fate had finally been sealed. Could anybody imagine him as a planter in the United States or taking tea with elderly English ladies? The legend that surrounded him would have been destroyed. He had to be martyred."[1]

These lines of Tulard establish an evident separation between the historic legacy of Napoleon's work and the echoes of a legend. And since the legend, separated in part from the work—be it lofty or criminal—is nourished by the meteoric parabola of a career, one could see in the Napoleonic legend the immediate model and the simple explanation for the attraction Hitler's "persona" exercises on today's imagination.

It could be that this is partially so, but in my eyes this fascination, which forms the central axis of the new discourse on Nazism, was nourished on another soil.

For what distinguished the attractive power of Napoleon from that of Hitler is the difference between a career one knows, however confusedly, is linked to a life's work, and a trajectory that could only land in a void. A force came out of nothing and ended in nothing, after having accumulated an extraordinary power, unleashed a war without parallel, committed crimes heretofore beyond imagination—a force that hacked the world to pieces in order to founder in nothingness.

That essential nihilism very soon formed the mystery zone of Hitler's image.* But simultaneously, especially after the end of World War II, an extraordinary eagerness for details of the Führer's personal life inflamed a mass audience. Valets, secretaries, press attachés, military aides, childhood friends, companions from the Vienna men's shelter, foreign diplomats, generals, party dignitaries—each one flung his testimony into the complacent ear of a public that wanted to know everything: the color of Hitler's bootlaces, the thickness of his glasses, the specifics of his sex life, the fits of rage, the taste for opera, the love of art, his graphic talent, his dietary practices, his fear of illness, his work habits, the monologues, his love of tidbits, of dogs, of blond children, of large convertibles, of whips, etc. It is against this double background that Albert Speer's memoirs appeared, a generation after the war was over. Despite all the reservations, the fascination, which until that

*In the 1930s, that was the interpretation of Hitler given by a Hermann Rauschning, the ex-gauleiter of Danzig *(The Revolution of Nihilism: Warning to the West)*, or of Konrad Heiden, his first biographer. The same thesis of an essential nihilism was taken up again by Alan Bullock in his great postwar biography *Hitler: A Study in Tyranny* (New York: Harper & Row, 1953).

moment no one had dared name, would again find a voice.

"The image of Adolf Hitler as the tribune of the people," Speer writes, "despite the innumerable details accumulated in my memory, is still for me a totally baffling image and one that I cannot specify in any definite fashion. I lack the distance of someone who has not taken part."[2]

In fact—and Speer admits it—Hitler's magic hold forms the leitmotiv, the one continuous element in their relationship. The Führer's favorite architect become his minister of armaments, one of the most intelligent people in his entourage, was, like the others, subject to that spell to the very end. Remembering a scene in 1943, he notes that "a word from Hitler had lost none of its magical force. To be precise, all the intrigues and struggles for power were directed toward eliciting such a word, or what it stood for. The position of each and everyone of us was dependent on his attitude."[3] This emotional bondage was maintained from the beginning to the end.

The day after Hitler's suicide is announced, Speer, unpacking his suitcase in Doenitz's headquarters, discovers a red leather case containing a portrait of the Führer that his secretary had put there. He places the photograph on the table and is shaken by tears: "Only now was the spell broken, the magic extinguished."[4]

The intimate character of this portrait and its frame is striking. Perhaps the secretary had indeed put it there, but in order for her to do so it must have had a central place on the minister's desk or in his apartment.

These are signs of a deep attachment only death can end. "His magic charm had stopped working."

In Speer's memoirs, what is the element that induces the effect? What is the ingredient of this new fascination that is to be developed in the new discourse? The juxtaposition, indeed the fusion, of the daily aspects of Hitler's life and of the image of this power of nothingness. I propose to show that this fascination is of the same kind as the aesthetic hold discussed in the preceding chapter. There it was kitsch and death, here it is the more and more frequent display of a Hitler who is Everyman, himself wrapped in kitsch, and at the same time the image of an almost superhuman power flung into emptiness. And here, too, we will confront the evidence. The structure of this contemporary fascination seems to correspond in many ways to the hold of the past.

Hitler's everyday face reappears in the new discourse haloed by the sentimental kitsch that plays such a decisive role in our interpretation of the total phenomenon. The procedure is not always clear at first sight, for what sometimes appears as a seemingly neutral detail is in fact pushed into obsession:

> On April 20, 1889, a gray Saturday when the temperature was 7 degrees Centigrade and the humidity 89%, at six-thirty in the evening, on the eve of Easter, the Austrian couple Aloïs and Klara Hitler had a son at the Pomeranian Inn in Braunau. . . .

This is how Werner Maser begins his biography of the future leader of Germany. He continues:

Two days later, on Easter Monday at three-fifteen—at the nearby Linzer Landestheater, Millöcker's operetta *Das Verschwundene Schloss* [*The Vanished Castle*], including a song very popular in Austria, "A bisserl Lieb, a bisserl Treu" ("A bit of Love, a Bit of Trust") had just begun—the Catholic priest of Braunau, Ignaz Probst, baptized the child Adolf Hitler.[5]

Now, such precision is not merely casual. It creates an atmosphere of profound intimacy by appealing to the smallest concrete detail. But it is an intimacy that envelops both the reader and the subject in a subtle halo of legend. They are transported into an enchanted place with its village inn, Easter evening, an operetta that sings of love and fidelity, the melancholy of a gray afternoon, and, to be sure, the family idyll: father, mother, and the newborn. One is reminded of certain scenes in Syberberg's film, particularly the Christmas broadcast.

Much stranger, but sketched according to the same rules—although the presentation is more direct—is the fictional Hitler in George Steiner's recent novel *The Portage to San Cristóbal of A.H.*[6] The time is the 1970s, and the Führer is alive. After years of unremitting search, a group of Israeli agents (guided from a distance by Lieber, their mysterious chief) have penetrated into the Brazilian jungle, to the heart of darkness, and there they find him: a decrepit old man squatting in the middle of the Amazonian forest. It was a double who had died thirty years ago in the ruins of the Chancellery.

The return voyage begins. Encountering fearful difficulties, the small group takes the old man toward San Cristóbal, where perhaps there will be a means of transporting him to Israel for trial. The death of one member of the team, the exhaustion of the others, and the increasingly uncertain conditions of the trip force them to stop. Hitler will be judged where they are.

In the first scene in which he appears physically on the road back, he falls in the mud and then, with his good arm, points to a snake. The symbolism is unequivocal. And when the old man opens his mouth for the first time, he says: "Music, music . . . Let me hear the music. I haven't heard music. Oh in a long time. Many years perhaps. . . . It is a long time since I have heard a woman sing."[7] Perhaps it is impossible to evoke a fictional Hitler without associations of this kind adhering to the portrait much as the slime of the Amazonian swamp sticks to his face. . . . But it is in Syberberg, in Fassbinder, and in Speer himself that one finds Hitler's ordinariness pushed to the extreme limits of kitsch.

The Christmas Eve sequence in Syberberg's film, where the valet Krause shares with us his memories, brings to the surface the most archaic legends and our most deep-rooted dreams of childhood. Hitler is the hidden prince of legend who runs through the streets of the town dressed as a poor man, the humble toad whom the princess finds, the poor man who knocks at the door of the house at night asking for shelter. He is the great detective disguised as a simple passerby, as the waiter in a café perhaps. Now, in all legends, in all dreams, there is the incandescent moment of discovery that provides the true frisson. The toad suddenly becomes a prince, the detective removes his disguise—all of us have imagined ourselves the prince or the detective at the moment of triumph. The juxtaposition of the human and the ordinary with evoked or implicit great power necessarily leads to a magic moment of revelation.

We lack a phenomenology of compassion. Krause tells us:

> For many years, it was impossible to get him to wear colored shoes with light-colored suits. During the first three years, he basically wore black silk or lisle stockings and black patent-leather half-shoes with his light-colored suits. With the stockings, he always had something to complain about, for they were usually too short, so they supposedly slid down his calves. He would then exclaim: "Isn't it possible for the Führer of the German people to get a pair of decent socks?" Frau Kannenberg and I combed all the stores in Berlin.
>
> The black shoes with the colored suits were an atrocity. But here too he became sensible only after several years. . . .[8]

This great man who made and unmade history, unable to match socks and suits! This is the side of "the genius disarmed by the problems of everyday life" or the "naïve child," which, under the circumstances, upsets the midinette. Compassion is born here for the hero's vulnerability to the small things in life. The spectator identifies with what he sees, and feels superior, for he knows how to pick the right socks. When Hitler exclaims "Isn't it possible for the Führer of the German people to get a pair of decent socks?" it is chalked up against him. The spectator knows that the reproach is unjustified—it is he, the Führer, who does not know how to choose proper socks, and he has only himself to blame. But this double weakness is pardoned twice over.

In *Lili Marleen,* Willie, whose refrain is about to begin to conquer every battlefield and every heart, finds herself in the office of Hinkel, Goebbels's aide. He makes a sexual overture to her. She refuses, and he threatens her. Suddenly someone enters with the news that the Führer wishes to meet Lili Marleen tomorrow at five o'clock for tea. Hinkel is left openmouthed. "The Führer?" One can feel a wave of satisfaction pass through the theater. On the point of conquering Stalingrad, devising the fall of the British Empire, the Führer, who will soon dominate the world, taking an interest in a small-time singer and her little song of love and nostalgia.

Hitler's passion for architecture adds a special dimension to this familiarity, to this engaging aspect of his personality. What, in effect, can be more moving than the master of the Third Reich's genuine artistic interest, his love of detail, his astonishing professional knowledge, the priority granted by the leader of the German nation to the examination of architectural blueprints, to discussions of facades and staircases, to a projected museum? What is more touching than his dreams of rebuilding Linz, the city of his childhood, at a time when everything else around him is beginning to collapse? Before the war, his close associates knew that discussion of urgent business would be at an end the moment Speer would arrive with his architectural drawings. He was therefore sometimes asked to hide them in the telephone switchboard. But Hitler was not always fooled. He would go himself to look for the rolls of drawings and plans.[9] This is the mischievous little boy who refuses to do his homework and runs off to play with his electric train.

What impassioned Hitler the most was the model of the future imperial capital. It was set up in the old exhibition halls of the Academy of Fine Arts and linked to the new Reich Chancellery. Sometimes, late at night, the Führer invited his guests to follow him. Equipped with flashlights and keys, they set out. In the empty rooms, spotlights lit up the models. "There was no need for me to do the talking," Speer adds, "for Hitler, with flashing eyes, explained every single detail to his companions."[10]

Still another edifying scene: Paris has fallen. The next day Hitler is in the French capital surrounded by his generals, Speer at his side. Instead of a grand parade down the Champs-Elysées or a triumphal tour of the conquered city, Hitler prefers a tourist visit to the Opera. He knows all the nooks and crannies, and guides his entourage through the building, accompanied by an old, white-haired member of the custodial staff. At one point he remarks that a salon seems to have disappeared. The attendant confirms it: The room was removed several years ago during a renovation. "There, you see how well I know my way about,"[11] Hitler says with satisfaction. On the day after his most brilliant victory, the Gröfaz (*Grösster Feldherr aller Zeiten*—the greatest military chief of all time) is carried away by his passion for architecture!

But gradually, as the war lengthened and the defeats increased, Hitler isolated himself more and more and retired into himself. In the autumn of 1943, when he still dominated the Continent from the Atlantic to the Don and from Cap Nord to Greece, he says to Speer: "One day I will have only two friends left: Fräulein Braun and my dog."

Terror and pity, the two provinces of tragedy. Later, when he is burrowed in his bunker, the former master of the continent sees his closest paladins, Göring and Himmler, betray him. Several of the faithful are still there: Bormann, Goebbels and his family, Ribbentrop, Eva Braun, and the dog. Speer is about to depart. Hitler talks calmly about his forthcoming suicide: "Fraulein Braun wants to depart this life with me, and I'll shoot Blondi [the dog] beforehand. Believe me, Speer, it is easy for me to end my life. A brief moment and I'm freed of everything, liberated from this painful existence."[12]

The emphasis that the new discourse has put on scenes from everyday life, tinted with all the reflections of kitsch, does in fact correspond to a real composite of the Hitler image as it was presented and broadcast during the "conquest of power" and under the Third Reich, at least until the last two years of the war. Of the four men who directed the destiny of the world during the period between the great economic depression and the end of World War II, none but Hitler cultivated an image of the petty bourgeois Mr. Everyman, the middle-class common denominator throughout the West. Churchill remained an aristocrat and Roosevelt a patrician, and Stalin, the little father of the people, cloaked himself in steadily increasing mystery, avoiding great public events and direct contact with the masses.

The color movies of everyday life at the Berghof and the photo albums assembled with such care by Heinrich

Hoffman, the Führer's personal photographer, are full of images of bourgeois serenity: Hitler with Goebbels's or Speer's blond children, with his dog Blondi, with Eva Braun. Everyone knows of the Führer's taste for sweets and cream cakes, for sentimental films, adventure stories and operettas. He was gallant to fashionable actresses, whom he enjoyed inviting to the Berghof for tea, the invitation that Fassbinder evokes in *Lili Marleen*. In the eyes of the masses, Hitler appeared neither a solemn monarch nor a mysterious tyrant, neither as representative of an elite habituated to the burden of power nor as toiling servant of the state risen from the ranks. Hitler, as has been said so often, is the projection of tastes and desires most broadly accepted in his times. With one exception.

Along with the decor of bourgeois kitsch appears the simultaneous surge of nothingness. And this juxtaposition of kitsch and nothingness creates the singular effect of the new discourse on Hitler and represents the basis of the extraordinary frenzy he created in his lifetime.

Nevertheless, one has the impression that in some contemporary works on Hitler there is some hesitation concerning this aspect of absolute destruction. Thus, in Joachim Fest's 1973 biography of Hitler, one feels a doubt: Is Hitler only a destroyer? Hasn't he left a body of work behind him? "Recorded history presents no other phenomenon that resembles him," says Fest, "but can he be considered great?" This is the question with which the book opens.

Fest speculates that had Hitler been killed in an accident or assassination at the end of 1938, he would have been considered one of the greatest German statesmen, a man who had fulfilled German history. The aggressiveness of his speeches and of *Mein Kampf,* his anti-Semitism, his vision of world domination probably would have been forgotten; one would have talked about only utopian projects, necessarily linked to the beginning of a career. But his last six and a half years took that glory from him. And Fest, again picking up the question "Ought we to call him 'great'?"[13] attempts an answer in his conclusion.

One obstacle has now been eliminated, he tells us, since time has allowed us to overcome the shadow of the death camps; one can thus talk about what Nazism was really about.[14] Hitler was indeed the architect of a great work because of his desperate defense of Europe's right to remain mistress of her history and destiny; because he championed the "middle road" of a middle class that wanted neither capitalism nor, above all, Marxism, that deliberately placed itself between right and left, East and West; because of his revolutionary modernization, which, for a time at least, shattered the Marxist revolution;[15] because of his desire to integrate the "apolitical" Germans into the political process. In short, Hitler was the creator of the German political consciousness. . . .[16]

But in the very last lines of the book, Fest again hesitates and takes up the theme of nothingness:

Since he could not offer any persuasive picture of the future state of the world, any hope, any encouraging goal, nothing of his thought survived him. He had always used ideas merely as instruments; when at death he abandoned them, they were compromised and used up. This great demagogue left behind him not so much as a memorable phrase, an impressive formula. Similarly, he who had wanted to be the greatest builder of all time left not a single building to the present. Nothing survived. . . . Hitler had no secret that extended beyond his immediate present. The people whose loyalty and admiration he had won never followed a vision, but only a force. In retrospect his life seems like a steady unfolding of tremendous energy. Its effects were vast, the terror it spread enormous; but when it was over, there was little left for the memory to hold.[17]

In an interview with Alain de Benoist, Fest presents the same hesitation on another level of reasoning: "Hitler was a very great man because the component of evil was very great in him."[18]

Historical grandeur unfurls beyond good and evil:

For world history is not played out in the area that is "the true site of morality," and Burckhardt has also spoken of the "strange exemption from the ordinary moral code" which we tend to grant in our minds to great individuals. We may surely ask whether the absolute crime of mass extermination planned and committed by Hitler is not of an utterly different nature, overstepping the bounds of the moral context recognized by both Hegel and Burckhardt.[19]

However, the phenomenon of the great man is primarily aesthetic, Fest adds, again taking up Burckhardt's formulation. And, at precisely this level, he seems to decide that Hitler does not correspond to the aesthetic canons of greatness, and that therefore he cannot qualify as great.[20] Ultimately only the nothingness remains.

But the representation of this all-destructive force is ambiguous in some texts and takes on a quasi-metaphysical dimension in others, thus revealing attraction much more than horror, seduction much more than repulsion. Speer writes in his prison journals:

> I would unhesitatingly say that fire was Hitler's proper element. Though what he loved about fire was not its Promethean aspect but its destructive force. That he set the world aflame and brought fire and sword upon the Continent—such statements may be mere imagery. But fire itself, literally and directly, always stirred a profound excitement in him. I recall his ordering showings in the Chancellery of the films of burning London, of the sea of flames over Warsaw, of exploding convoys, and the rapture with which he watched those films. I never saw him so worked up as toward the end of the war, when in a kind of delirium he pictured for himself and for us the destruction of New York in a hurricane of fire. He described the skyscrapers being turned into gigantic burning torches, collapsing upon one another, the glow of the exploding city illuminating the dark sky.[21]

Syberberg's film uses apocalyptic themes when it deals with the end of civilization, the end of the world, or even the end of the universe, as necessary accompaniment to his interpretation of Hitler; and in George Steiner's novel, the theme of destruction and nothingness seems to enhance the very nature of this false Messiah, who, holder of the power of the Word like the Creator himself, can, by the Word, "unmake" or destroy all of creation: "Where God said, let there be, he will unsay. And there is *one* word . . . *one* word amid the million sounds that make the secret sum of all language, which if spoken in hatred may end creation, as there was one that brought creation into being."[22]

Now, a part of the exaltation of the masses during the Nazi era came from that mania for destruction that shook Hitler, from that fever of nothingness. On October 18, 1944, Ernst Jünger noted in his journal:

Kniébolo's [the author's code name for Hitler] radio appeal for the formation of Volkssturm batallions for the extermination measures directed against the people. All of his inspirations have proved to be experiments, which were then used in large measure against the Germans. I think of blowing up synagogues, the extermination of the Jews, the bombing of London, the flying bombs, and other things. He shows first of all that such deeds are thinkable and possible, destroys the safeguards and gives the masses an opportunity for agreement. *The frenetic applause that accompanied his appearance was the agreement for self-destruction, a highly nihilistic act.* * My horror stems from having heard it from the beginning: the monstrous applause for the Pied Piper music. Of course, Kniébolo is also a European phenomenon. Germany as the center will always be the place where such things are visible first and most sharply.[23]

The accomplishment of destruction was even more continuous, more systematic, than these lines of Jünger's would suggest, an accomplishment known to many, an obvious ingredient in the ecstasy and the acclamations of a significant part of the population.

*My emphasis.

71

Oranienburg and Dachau; the Gestapo cellars on Prinz-Albrechtstrasse and the SA massacre; the disappearance of political opponents and the burning of synagogues; the exclusion of Jews from every sphere of German life; the invasion of Poland and the attacks on Warsaw, Rotterdam, and Coventry; the evacuation of the Jews to the east and the consequent horrible rumors; the disappearance of the mentally ill and the photographs of the charnel houses that circulated in the Reich; what was said in passing by rail in the proximity of Auschwitz and the anticipated annihilation of London; the meat hooks reserved for the plotters of July 20, 1944, and the order to destroy Germany itself—all this, and nevertheless it was only on May 1, 1945, that Hitler's magic charm stopped for Speer.

Thus we are here confronted with the two sides of Hitler: that of yesterday and that of today; with the facts and with their reinterpretation; with reality and with its aesthetization. On the one hand, the approachable human being, Mr. Everyman enveloped in kitsch; on the other, that blind force launched into nothingness. Each side did attract, and, for some, as I try to show, the attraction continues to operate today. The coexistence of these two aspects, their juxtaposition, their simultaneous and alternating presence is, it seems to me, the true source of this spell. At the end of this essay, it will be necessary to explain this point, to interpret it within a general historical context; let it suffice here to take up again a picture that presents the one side of Hitler and the other, in order to show briefly several immediate aspects of this fusion.

There is in Speer's memoirs a photograph with the

following caption: "Hitler directed his wars, often for months, from the Obersalzberg. After meetings we never failed to take a daily walk to the tea pavilion. Hitler was generally taciturn. Often we walked side by side without saying a word, each one plunged in his own thoughts."*

The general background is one of a winter day, no doubt near the end of the afternoon, according to the caption and the falling light reflected in the picture. The mountain landscape is blurred, covered with deep snow. The upper half of the picture shows a snowy sky where indistinct clouds gradually pass from white to gray. The immediate impact is one of melancholy, even of desolation. And here, in this frame, the two silhouettes in the foreground. They were photographed from behind, and in fact one can see only two black shapes detached from the whitish background of the snow and the sky. Clearly, they are not talking. They walk, as the caption says, side by side, without saying a word, each one plunged in his own thoughts.

All the elements of a kitsch representation can be immediately perceived: the great man's solitude, the silent fidelity of his gallant companion, and the accumulated signs of desolation. Speer and Hitler, walking through a countryside without another living soul in it, appear to be advancing into absolute solitude, toward nothingness, as the picture strongly suggests. Here, then, are reunited the two sources of fascination. The power of evocation here is not entirely different, it seems to me, from that of the Dürer engraving that be-

*This photograph can be found in the group of pictures following page 406 of *Inside the Third Reich.*

came one of the ideal representations of romanticism
and German nationalism: the knight riding between
death and the devil. We are at the sources of the romantic frisson, at the sources at once of kitsch and of nihilism. One has often heard talk of the attractions of fascist or Nazi pessimism; we are not far, here, from some
of its deepest roots.

Some important present-day reinterpretations have
taken this fascination as a central theme without the
personage of Hitler being directly concerned. Substi-
tutes for him are utilized, and generally the seduction
takes an openly erotic form. But it seems to me that this
new dimension is only a variant of the elements presented thus far.

During the Seventies, with the release of the films *The
Night Porter* and *Lacombe Lucien,* after the impact of
The Damned and *The Ogre,* and with the appearance,
finally, everywhere in the West, of a vast pornographic
output centered on Nazism, this aspect of the Nazi fascination elicited a number of diverse interpretations.

"Power carries an erotic charge," said Michel Foucault in an interview with *Cahiers du cinéma.*

> This poses a historical problem: How could Nazism,
> which was represented by lamentable, shabby, puritan
> young men, by a species of Victorian spinsters, have
> become everywhere today—in France, in Germany, in
> the United States—in all the pornographic literature of
> the whole world, the absolute reference of eroticism? All
> the shoddiest aspects of the erotic imagination are now
> put under the sign of Nazism. . . .[24]

And this eroticization of power is not uniquely a post-war phantasm. Foucault concedes that Nazi power was in its time profoundly adulated:

> Nazism never gave a pound of butter to the people, it never gave anything but power. Nevertheless, one has to ask oneself why, if the regime was nothing else but this bloody dictatorship, there were Germans up to May 8, 1945, who fought to the last drop of blood, unless there had been some kind of attachment to the people in power. . . .[25]

In fact, Michel Foucault makes a statement rather than giving an explanation, but his statement sums up one of the essential difficulties facing those interpretations of Nazism that take into account only the play of economic forces or of political calculations.

The historic explanation for Nazism must be understood on very diverse levels. But to understand the phantasms that underlay many Germans' relationship to Hitler, the frenzy of their applause, their attachment to him until the last moment, it is necessary to take into account their perverse rapport with a chief and a system for reasons that certainly were not explicit and would not have shown in an opinion poll: the yearning for destruction and death. Some people have difficulty making the connection, a difficulty, which, for example, gives Michel Foucault's interview with *Cahiers du cinéma* the character of a dialogue of the deaf.

FOUCAULT: What is it that makes power desirable and really desired? It is easy to see the procedures that transmit and reinforce this eroticization. But for the eroticization to take hold, those who are attached to power and have accepted it must already be erotic.

CAHIERS: That's much more difficult since the representation of power is rarely erotic. De Gaulle or Hitler were not particularly seductive.

FOUCAULT: Yes, and I have to ask myself if in the Marxist analyses one is not a little bit the victim of the abstract character of the notion of freedom.[26]

The psychological dimension of Nazism's hold is not denied, even by the *Cahiers,* but contained within certain limits compatible with accepted political explanation:

> Fascism never signified the liberation of sexual desire, at least its conscious liberation, but, quite the contrary, appealed to moral rigor, to propriety, to health through physical exercise and military training, etc. . . . None of this was ever very Nietzschean, and it is truly a tour de force on Madame Cavani's part to share with everybody her belief that Nazism was this mad amorous generosity. However, it doesn't need much thought to see that Hitler and Goebbels are not figures of ravaging desire.[27]

The fact is that under Nazism Hitler was indeed the object of desire, not necessarily the actual person—although the influence of his oratory still has to be discussed—but the idealized image of the chief expressing both a universal sentimentality and the attraction to nothingness that sometimes seizes contemporary crowds. In current representations of Nazism or works

that in one way or another reevoke this erotic fascination, the object of desire is most often a subordinate,
often someone who belongs or belonged to the SS, and,
in *Lacombe Lucien,* an ordinary French auxiliary of the
Gestapo. *But no matter what the rank of the object of
desire, it is the whole system that is sketched into the
background, the system and the values it embodies.*

One might argue that *The Night Porter* and *Lacombe
Lucien* intend to show the exact opposite—the triumph
of love and desire despite the obstacles imposed by the
past or ideology or morality or the system. That might
have been the intention of the directors, but it seems
clear to me that for a good number of viewers the erotic
relationship shown on the screen creates a special
problem precisely because of the background, just because Max or Lucien represents Nazism and collaboration, not in spite of that fact. That Max will oppose real
Nazis, that he has become a repentant Nazi, if you will,
or that Lucien never did understand the real situation,
doesn't change, it seems to me, the associations that are
imposed. Besides, if it were clear that Max couldn't
conjure up Nazism, or Lucien collaboration, where
would the ambiguity noticed by many critics be, and,
indeed, the problem?

Thus, the erotic dimension of this fascination has
many components. On the first level, an erotic relationship of a female (Lucia or France) who symbolizes the
victims with a man identified with the hangman has all
the force of desire despite ideology. On the second
level, the relationship is sustained, at least for the
viewer, by the implicit symbolic assets both sides bring
to the situation, especially so in the case of the man.

Some spectators will be repelled, others attracted, whether they admit the attraction or not. The attraction, moreover, does not depend only on the situation shown in the film, but on the unsaid or barely said aspects of the backround. There is also the frequent utilization of effects and themes on this second level, which I have analyzed in these pages as a kind of necessary adjunct of the intrigue, adding all the nuances of aesthetic power to the erotic themes brought out in the story.

It is the mix of these various levels that creates in the viewer of *The Night Porter,* of *Lacombe Lucien,* of *The Damned,* too, as well as in the reader of *The Ogre,* that malaise so often difficult to grasp. One looks for it on one level and it turns up on another; one looks for it in the theme, in the problems posed, and it is in the aesthetic. And thus the aesthetic dimension of the fascination, which one attributes to the various works, results after all in a particular aesthetization of an erotic plane, in an aesthetization leading us at once to our basic structure (kitsch as foundation of this aesthetic and death haloing the principal personages, death as central theme and result of each of the stories) and thus to the general sources of the Nazi hold. For what is said about the reflections of Nazism seems to me true for Nazism itself. Given the erotic charge of Nazi power, the erotic attachment to Hitler, this could be, for some, a true love relationship. But it seems to me—as I have tried to show in the preceding pages—that the foundations of this influence are broader, making them both more plausible and easier to integrate into an attempt at global interpretation.

78

In the last pages of the preceding chapter, I tried to show how much the very structure of the language about Nazism—as of the Nazi language itself—reinforces two series of contradictory themes forming the aesthetic power of Nazism. Here, a return to the function of language is necessary, for language was always the decisive component of Hitler's influence; not what Hitler said but the way in which he said it. Speer, Fest, and Syberberg grant Hitler's word a promordial role, reflecting the view of the times. But it is in George Steiner's novel that this aspect takes on an almost metaphysical import:

> As it is written in the learned Nathaniel of Mainz: there shall come upon the earth in the time of night a man surpassing eloquent. . . . When He made the Word, God made possible also its contrary. . . . No, He created on the night side of language a speech for hell. Whose words mean hatred and vomit of life. Few men can learn that speech or speak it for long. It burns their mouths. It draws them into death. But there shall come a man whose mouth shall be as a furnace and whose tongue as a sword laying waste. He will know the grammar of hell and teach it to others. He will know the sounds of madness and loathing and make them seem music. Where God said, let there be, he will unsay.[28]

The testimonies on this subject cannot be counted anymore: Through his words, Hitler holds crowds under his spell, hypnotizes his entourage, paralyzes his domestic enemies, subjugates his foreign opponents; through his words, he establishes his power and provokes destruction. But here a paradox intervenes, a sudden contradiction. Steiner's thesis giving Hitler's word the central role in the ultimate destruction, that of the Jews, is no longer confirmed by the facts. Here Hitler's other face, the face of silence, stands revealed. When we approach the final, irrevocable dividing line, the point of total rupture and no return—the decision to exterminate the Jews of Europe down to the last one— we are confronted only by silence.

Eight months before the war began, Hitler told the Reichstag: "If the Jews are responsible for a new war . . . the result will be the extermination of the Jews." Once again words; at the time only words. No decision seems to have been taken. For another two years the threats delivered in the Reichstag are not yet policy. Then comes the decision, in silence; the setting in motion of the machine of destruction, in silence; the end, in silence. Not even words written in an order, nothing. Not even the direct evidence of an oral order. We have many indirect proofs of Hitler's intervention in the Final Solution and a number of references to his orders, coming mostly from Himmler.* But, from Hitler himself, we have only some laconic remarks to one or another of his intimates. Also, a few sinister allusions in the Reichstag, but vague like those of September or November 1942.

"You will remember the session of the Reichstag when I said: If by chance the Jews imagine they could wage international war to eliminate the European

---

*See Gerald Fleming, *Hitler und die Endlösung* (Munich: Limes Verlag, 1982). American translation: *Hitler and the Final Solution* (Berkeley: University of California Press, 1984).

races, the result will be not the elimination of the European races but that of the Jews in Europe. Some mocked my prophecies. Among those who laughed yesterday, many are silent now, and those who still laugh will perhaps stop soon."

That's all. Sinister hints, horrifying in what is left unsaid, what is left to the imagination. Compare them to the flow of justifications following the liquidation of Roehm and his friends, to any of his foreign-policy initiatives, or to any stage of the war. Brief passages in a speech, no more than the muted accompaniment of silence.

3

"Will we ever become free of the oppressive curse of guilt if we do not get at the center of it?" Hans-Jürgen Syberberg asks in the introduction to his film. He continues:

Yes, indeed, it is only in a film—the art of our times—a film that is precisely about this Hitler within us, from Germany, that hope may come at all. In the name of our future, we have to overcome and conquer him and thereby ourselves, and only here can a new identity be found through recognizing and separating, sublimating and working on our tragic past.[1]

A "work of mourning" *(Trauerarbeit)*—Syberberg first used this term in connection with his 1975 film devoted to Winifred Wagner, then also in describing his *Hitler*—a deliverance, a necessary exorcism. For some, a film like Syberberg's means total acceptance of the past and thus its definitive expulsion. For others, the endless transpositions and an aestheticism pushed to its extreme limits represent just so many defenses against reality, giving these attempts their ambiguous character. Here we are faced with one of the many aspects of exorcism.

I shall not speak of exorcism as a willingness to confront reality to the bitter end, but first of all of a confrontation that, at the same time, remains an evasion; of neutralization of the past, of concealment, voluntary or not, of what in this past has become unbearable. I shall speak mostly of what happens today. But strange as it may seem at first glance, even the Nazis knew about confronting reality and evading it at the same time.

It is worth repeating that the new discourse allows us to better understand the mechanisms of yesterday's fascination, to penetrate a reality that sometimes escapes us. But such indirect truth illuminating a still opaque phenomenon does not mean that on another level, that of the representation of certain events, one does not find oneself facing evident distortions, engendered, no doubt, by the need to exorcise the past precisely. Note that in *Lili Marleen* and in Truffaut's *The Last Métro*, for instance, the image projected is one of almost general opposition to Nazism and collaboration, inside the Reich and in France. In these films, true Nazis and true collaborators are rare and isolated, and the masses seem to have their heart in the right place.*

This type of analysis could be developed at length and a place found for most of the works mentioned so

---

*On this subject see François Garçon's excellent article "The return of a disturbing imposter: *Lili Marleen* and *Le Dernier Métro*," *Les Temps modernes,* 422 (September 1981): p. 539ff.

far, including Albert Speer's testimony,* Fest's biography, but above all Fest's film, *Hitler, eine Karriere (Hitler, a Career).* To multiply such examples would, however, mean a return to the accustomed debates. The purpose of this essay is different. So I will only very briefly cite some extreme examples of how facts are manipulated. These extremes reflect positions taken by a marginal group outside our field of discussion but who have received some attention. I am referring to the revisionists, who, in order to exorcise the past, have decided to deny all the evidence.

The basic positions of the revisionists have often been summarized. For example: "1. Hitler's 'gas chambers' never existed. 2. The 'genocide' (or attempted genocide) of the Jews never took place."[2] The proof? That poses no problem so long as all the testimony is challenged and all the evidence is considered false. This leads to the premise of the "nonexistence" of any trace of the extermination.

*Here is a brief example of the way Albert Speer obscures reality. We know that several of the accused in the July 20 plot to assassinate Hitler were hanged in such a way that strangulation was slow and the agony horrible. The executions were filmed and Hitler had them shown that same evening and, later, on several other occasions. Now here is how Speer remembers these events: "During these days a heap of photographs also lay on this table [the map table at the Rastenburg headquarters, S.F.]. Lost in thought, I picked one up, but quickly put it down. It was a picture of a hanged man in convict dress, a broad, colored stripe on his trousers. One of the SS leaders standing near me remarked, in explanation: 'That's Witzleben. Don't you want to see the others too? These are all photos of the executions.'

That evening the film of the execution of the conspirators was shown in the movie room. I could not and would not see it. . . . I saw many others going to this showing, mostly lower-ranking SS men and civilians. Not a single officer of the Wehrmacht attended." (*Inside the Third Reich*, p. 395.)

Not a word about the fact that the film had been prepared for Hitler and that he apparently took special pleasure in seeing it over and over again. About Speer's distortions, see the recent study by Mathias Schmidt, *Albert Speer: Das Ende eines Mythos* (Munich: Goldmann Wilhelm Verlag, 1983).

"A gassing cannot be improvised," Faurisson writes. "If the Germans had decided to gas millions of people, they would have needed a formidable machinery. It would have required a general order, which has never been found, examinations, studies, commands, plans that have never been seen. It would have required a collection of experts: architects, chemists, doctors, specialists in every kind of technology. It would have required releasing funds and distributing them, something which in a state like the Third Reich would have left many traces (we know down to the last penny how much the kennel at Auschwitz cost or the laurels ordered from the tree nursery). There would have been orders."[3]

That nothing holds in such arguments has been said over and over,* and there is no point here in joining that debate. It should suffice to add that even within the core of the revisionist theses there are "distinctions." Thus for Paul Rassinier there may well have been some extermination in gas chambers but nothing systematic and a lot less than people said.† According to the English revisionist David Irving, "the final solution" took place, but Hitler had nothing to do with it; everything was carried out secretly by Himmler and the SS.[4] Hellmut Diwald's position, finally, is more subtle because it seems to be in the mainstream, seems to take into account the complexities of history as well as the uncertainties that could surround this gloomiest chapter of

*On this subject, see Nadine Fresco, "Les Redresseurs des morts" (The rectifiers of the dead), *Les Temps modernes,* June 1980; Pierre Vidal-Naquet, "Un Eichmann de papier" (A paper Eichmann), *Esprit,* September 1980; Georges Wellers, *Les chambres à gaz ont existé (The Gas Chambers Existed)* (Paris: Gallimard, 1981).

†Paul Rassinier, *Le Mensonge d'Ulysse (The Lie of Ulysses)* (Paris: Librairie Française, 1955), p. 26.

modern times. What really happened in the camps? "That remains obscure [*ungeklärt*]"[5] Diwald writes, despite all the published material. All things considered, that's reassuring.

Revisionism purifies the past by trafficking in facts. At the opposite extreme, systematic historical research, which uncovers the facts in their most precise and most meticulous interconnection, also protects us from the past, thanks to the inevitable paralysis of language. That is the exorcism and *the involuntary evasion to which we are all subject* and whose mechanism has to be taken apart. Here is one text among others, a text many of us could have drafted:

> The first massacre of Jews deported from the Reich took place in November 1941. The Jews of some transports that had been diverted to the Reichskommissariat Ostland, mainly to Riga, Minsk and Kovno, were not assigned to the local ghettos or camps, as were the majority of the later transports; these Jews were shot upon arrival together with the local Jews in the executions already started by the Einsatzkommandos of the Security Police and the SD, as for instance in Riga on the so-called Bloody Sunday of November 30, 1941. At about the same time (November 1941), in the Reichsgau of Wartheland, the "Lange Special Commando" arrived in Chelmno (Kulmhof) and proceeded to construct temporary extermination facilities such as the gas vans of the type used by this commando during the euthanasia killings in the transit camp of Soldau, and as of December 1941 for the killing of Jews, mostly from the ghetto of Litzmannstadt. The idea that was initiated the previous summer in Posen, according to which the situation in the

ghetto could be relieved through the killing of Jews unable to work "by means of a quick-acting medium" had apparently fallen on fertile ground. The erection of Chelmno was intended mainly for this limited purpose —to make room for the second and third waves of Jewish transports from the Reich, which would be "temporarily" lodged in Litzmannstadt during the winter of 1941–42. The ghetto should be cleared of those unable to work (above all women and children), who would be brought to Chelmno for gassing. This action was mainly completed by the summer of 1942 (with the annihilation of about 100,000 Jews).[6]

A scholarly text such as this one makes the reader— sometimes himself a specialist—ask himself questions every scholarly text raises, those dealing with the accuracy of facts and their interconnection. In some ways the scholarly mind does not allow an emotional reaction. It is blocked and immediately replaced by a problem drawn from the text: Was it really the Lange Special Commando? Would it not instead have been X or Y? And how many Jews were directed toward Riga, how many others to Kovno, how many more to Minsk?

Then the real trap of language is unexpectedly sprung. Take several phrases from this text:

" . . . (A) The Jews of some transports . . . were not assigned to the local ghettos or camps. . . . (B) These Jews were shot upon arrival. . . ."

" . . . (A) At about the same time, the 'Lange Special Commando' arrived in Chelmno and (B) proceeded to construct temporary extermination facilities. . . . "

" ... (A) The ghetto should be cleared of those unable to work (above all, women and children), (B) who would be brought to Chelmno for gassing."

Here the unreality springs from an absolute disparity between the two halves of the phrases: The first half implies an ordinary administrative measure, and is put in totally normal speech; the second half accounts for the natural consequence, except that here, suddenly, the second half describes murder. The style doesn't change. It cannot change. It is in the nature of things that the second half of the text can only carry on the bureaucratic and detached tone of the first. That neutralizes the whole discussion and suddenly places each one of us, before we have had time to take hold of ourselves, in a situation not unrelated to the detached position of an administrator of extermination: Interest is fixed on an administrative process, an activity of building and transportation, words used for record-keeping. And that's all.

"(A) All the students of the primary schools in the departments of Seine and l'Essone were taken by bus to the camp of (X) near Fontainebleau and (B) machine-gunned in open-air trenches."

Behind each sentence, the habitual structures of imagination impose themselves to hide the bare significance of the words. Thus the activities of the "Lange Commando": "The 'Lange Special Commando' arrived in Chelmno and proceeded to construct temporary extermination facilities such as the gas vans of the type used by this commando during the euthanasia killings in the transit camp of Soldau, and as of December 1941 for the killing of the Jews, mostly from the ghetto of

Litzmannstadt." How is the story neutralized? Quite simply. Not just anybody is sent to Chelmno, but only specialists who have already worked in Soldau and then in Litzmannstadt—truck specialists ("Let's see his dossier. . . . Oh, well, he has already worked at Soldau . . . knows the type of truck perfectly, an excellent technician . . .").

There should be no misunderstanding about what I am trying to say: The historian cannot work in any other way, and historical studies have to be pursued along the accepted lines. The events described are what is unusual, not the historian's work. We have reached the limit of our means of expression. Others we do not possess.

"Languages have great reserves of life," George Steiner writes in *Language and Silence.*[7]

They can absorb masses of hysteria, illiteracy, and cheapness. . . . But there comes a breaking point. Use a language to conceive, organize, and justify Belsen; use it to make out specifications for gas ovens; use it to dehumanize man during twelve years of calculated bestiality. Something will happen to it. Make of words what Hitler and Goebbels and the hundred thousand *Untersturmführer* made: conveyors of terror and falsehood. Something will happen to the words. Something of the lies and sadism will settle in the marrow of the language. Imperceptibly at first, like the poisons of radiation sifting silently into the bone. But the cancer will begin, and the deep-set destruction. The language will no longer grow and freshen. It will no longer perform, quite as well as it used to, its two principal functions: the conveyance of humane order which we call law, and the communica-

92

tion of the quick of the human spirit which we call grace.[8]

But isn't there a need to be more precise? Nothing happened to everyday language, whether it was German, English, French, or Russian, and one can continue to sing about the butterflies and the flowers as if nothing happened. But there it is: It is no longer a matter of butterflies and flowers, and, one ascertains it, the inadequacy grows between language and certain events. That began well before Auschwitz, perhaps with the First World War, only to reach its culmination with Auschwitz. Besides, language attempted to stick to the event in emptying itself, step by step, of all subjectivity and all emotion, in emptying the subject also of all interiorization (be it the language of literature or of the social sciences). But events moved faster than language. Since Auschwitz, the distance between them seems insurmountable. And perhaps that distance protects us from the unbearable impact of the past.

In order to better understand that paralysis of language, the field of observation has to be enlarged, and the most general and, on the whole, most simple question asked: Is there a work of art, a work of literature, for example, that has been able, in a decisive way, to confront these events?

At the bottom of the last page of his novel *Mephisto,* Klaus Mann inserted the following note: "All persons in this book represent types, not portraits." It is much the same for most of the literary production dealing with Nazism. The actor Gustav Grundgens, Goering's protégé and director general of theater in Berlin, who served as Klaus Mann's model, appears in the novel only as a montage of all the weaknesses and imperfections of the arriviste carving out a place in Hitler's Germany. Nothing is there to make a convincing personality. Ernie in *The Last of the Just* and Abel Tiffauges in *The Ogre* are archetypical figures, not real men.

Germany before Nazism, Germany at the hour when Nazism struck, at the time of the Great Depression, for example, saw the flowering of an unforgettably authentic literature. The lower depths of Berlin grabbed us by the throat in Alfred Döblin's *Berlin-Alexanderplatz,* the despair of the unemployed haunts Hans Fallada's books, the last reflections of a society about to fall apart reappear in Christopher Isherwood and Erich Kästner. But when it came to evoking the Nazi period, reality disappeared. In *Dr. Faustus,* Thomas Mann does not touch on Nazism itself, but explores the roots of it.* I would agree with J. P. Stern that Leverkuehn's life only very partially refers to Nazism and has mainly to be understood within its own, independent frame of reference.[9] In *The Tin Drum,* the dwarf Oscar takes his drum and his strident voice only to the periphery of the Nazi phenomenon. As for Heinrich Böll's heroes, they are, in the end, only pale messengers of humane sentiments.

During our period, both the capitalist jungle and the Stalinist hell have produced literary characters of formidable verisimilitude. We can recognize the Herzogs, the Portnoys, and all the Babbitts of the world; the uni-

---

*Not everybody will agree with this interpretation; some will see in Leverkuehn's life a symbolic interpretation of Nazism itself. In my opinion, if that were the case, some very problematic aspects of Thomas Mann's position would have to be faced. On this, see Ronald Gray, *The German Tradition in Literature 1871–1945* (Cambridge, 1965), p. 223.

verse of the GPU prisons, of *The First Circle* and the Gulag, has given us its Denisovitch as well as its Matriona. But the terrain of the most extreme upheaval of our time, which remains a fixed point in the imagination of our epoch, provides us with only shadows or myths. Even Italian fascism produced works of real density— *Bread and Wine, Christ Stopped at Eboli, The Garden of the Finzi-Continis.* But again and again, only paralysis surrounds Nazism. Sometimes the dichotomy is striking within one work. In Hermann Broch's *The Tempter,* Mother Gison is drawn with stupendous strength, while Marius Ratti, the vagabond who recalls Hitler, is made of papier-mâché. And in George Steiner's novel, Hitler as a personality simply does not exist—until the final speech. One could continue the list and show how in Thomas Pynchon's *Gravity's Rainbow* or Anthony Burgess's *Powers of Darkness* an expanding imagination seems to curdle and produce only artificial characters to evoke Nazi Germany. And Brecht wrote one of his weakest plays about Hitler.

This is the blockage the new discourse has tried to overcome by attempting to free the language of film and literature; by giving free rein to the imaginary and to the phantasms; by reevoking an atmosphere, an aesthetic, a desire; by playing on all the facets of horror.

But there, as I have already mentioned in the Introduction, one falls into the trap of shifting the attention to the aesthetic element. Let me briefly dwell again on this type of "affect neutralization."

George Steiner or Hans-Jürgen Syberberg, to take the two most important examples, certainly do not aim at neutralizing the impact of past horror; they probably wish to heighten it by discarding realism. Susan Sontag clearly stresses the reasons for Syberberg's rejection of realism:

> To simulate atrocity convincingly is to risk making the audience passive, reinforcing witless stereotypes, confirming distance and creating frustration. Convinced that there is a morally (and aesthetically) correct way for a filmmaker to confront Nazism, Syberberg can make no use of any of the stylistic conventions of fiction that pass for realism. Neither can he rely on documents to show how it "really" was. Like its simulation as fiction, the display of atrocity in the form of photographic evidence risks being tacitly pornographic. . . .[10]

It could be pornographic, but it needn't: what about Alain Resnais' *Night and Fog* or, different although realistic too, Max Ophuls's *The Sorrow and the Pity?* And, in the field of the literary documentary, what about Rolf Hochhuth's recent *Eine Liebe in Deutschland (A Love in Germany)?* But the main point is not that of realism, it is the way interpretations, fiction, and metaphor are being used.

In my introduction I mentioned the problem of intellectual or aesthetic complacency, the trap of self-feeding rhetoric or of sheer camera virtuosity, the "perversity of brilliance," to use Norman Podhoretz's tag about Hannah Arendt's *Eichmann in Jerusalem.* Even more basically, perhaps, the issue is one of *indiscriminate word and image overload on topics that call for so much restraint, hesitation, groping,* on events we are so far from understanding. In the *New York Times* review of Syberberg's *Hitler,* Vincent Canby put it very aptly:

> Like the dopey student in *National Lampoon's Animal House,* who, as he smokes marijuana for the first time, is suddenly aware of the universe contained within the atoms of his own little finger, Mr. Syberberg is not one who quickly dismisses his own insight, whether good, bad, indifferent or secondhand. As Mr. Syberberg is a filmmaker who shoots on what's called a one-to-one basis—that is, who uses every bit of footage he shoots —he seems to be a poet who's never tossed out a bit of scrap paper on which he's scribbled a rotten line. *Our Hitler* (the title under which it was shown in New York) is a movie that demands to be described in terms that cancel themselves out. It is both too much and too little, too obvious and too muddled, too heavy and too frivolous. The 42-year-old West German director, who appears to have poured his heart and soul into this film, is clearly a passionate man, but he is also woefully undiscriminating when it comes to evaluating his own work. . . .
>
> At one point in *Our Hitler* he doesn't hesitate to draw a parallel between M-G-M's butchery of Erich von Stroheim's original 42-reel version of *Greed* and the Nazi program to exterminate the Jews. To see such a parallel is not only to misuse history, but also to get it slightly wrong. After Mr. von Stroheim's battles with M-G-M about *Greed,* the M-G-M butchers hired him back to direct his classic screen version of *The Merry Widow.* . . .[11]

The endless stream of words and images becomes an ever more effective screen hiding the past, when the

only open avenue may well be that of quietness, simplicity, of the constant presence of the unsaid, of the
constant temptation of silence: "As rarely before,"
George Steiner writes in *Language and Silence,* "poetry
is tempted by silence."[12] Or this: "The best now, after
so much has been set forth, is, perhaps, to be silent; not
to add the trivia of literary sociological debate, to the
unspeakable. . . ."[13] There may be no rules, but doesn't
one feel the urge for some kind of parsimony, couldn't
one agree with Steiner's words? Not, however, with the
author of *The Portage to San Cristóbal of A.H.* but with
the author of *Language and Silence.*

It is on purpose that I avoid dealing with holocaust
literature itself; it would take me too far from the basic
aim of this essay: the new discourse on Nazism. Let me
just quote, parenthetically, a few lines from David
Stern's "Imagining the Holocaust," where, in reviewing
Lawrence L. Langer's *The Holocaust and the Literary
Imagination* and after mentioning the works of Ladislav
Fuks, Ilse Aichinger, and Jakov Lind, he adds:

> In all these works—and in some thirteen others, includ-
> ing the poetry of Paul Celan and Nelly Sachs, the novels
> of Pierre Gascar, Jerzy Kosinski, André Schwarz-Bart,
> Heinrich Böll, and Jorge Semprun—Langer shows how
> art, in confronting the Holocaust, ultimately turns into a
> kind of anti-art: the devices of narrative itself are finally
> exposed as inadequate to the atrocities. Lacking re-
> course to the cathartic resolution of tragedy, these books
> deliberately leave their readers in a state of uncertainty
> —is what they depict real or fantasy or fiction? As
> Langer remarks, many of the novels themselves resist

aesthetic form: through their rough edges, the historical atrocity persistently seeps in. . . .[14]*

Which is just another statement about the inadequacy of art and about realism versus aesthetization.

Let me come back now to some other aspects of exorcism. In his film, Syberberg picks up the film *M*'s famous monologue, that of the strangler of children:

Always, always, it drives me through the streets, and I always feel that someone's after me, and that's myself, and he . . . follows me relentlessly, but it was *me*, yes, yes. Sometimes I feel as if I'm running after myself. But it's impossible. I . . . have to obey. . . . I . . . have to get away . . . but the ghosts follow me. The ghosts of mothers, children, they're always there . . . and then I can, except, except, when I . . . do it. Then I see the posters, then I see the posters . . . Then I read what I've done, and I read, and . . . did I do that? . . .[15]

*In fact, I would agree with Leslie Epstein when he writes: "I have come, finally and reluctantly, to the conclusion that almost any honest eyewitness testimony of the Holocaust is more moving and more successful at creating a sense of what it must have been like in the ghettos and the camps than almost any fictional account of the same events. I am not sure why this should be so. It is not true of any other period in history. . . . More time, it seems, will have to pass before we are free enough to imagine the facts. Meanwhile, we do have . . . in hundreds of books of their own, the plain speech of the witnesses." (Leslie Epstein, "The Reality of Evil," *Partisan Review,* 4 [1976]: 639–40). But then, strangely enough, Leslie Epstein went on to write *King of the Jews* (New York: Coward, McCann & Geoghegan, 1979), reversing himself in the same way as George Steiner, who after *Language and Silence,* produced *The Portage to San Cristobal of A.H.* On Leslie Epstein's novel and this whole issue, see Alvin H. Rosenfeld's excellent piece "The Holocaust as Entertainment," *Midstream,* October 1979, pp. 55 seq. "After reading this novel," writes Rosenfeld, "one wishes the author had maintained the integrity of his own best insights and kept silent." Much more significant and no less problematic than Epstein's novel is William Styron's *Sophie's Choice.* For a strong critique of that novel, from the point of view taken here, see Rosenfeld's "The Holocaust According to William Styron," *Midstream,* December 1979.

What does *M* represent in Syberberg's film? Germany? Himmler and the SS? Hitler? All of us? If *M* symbolizes the destroyer, isn't he only a deranged man? Aren't we protected because the source of evil is exceptional and isolated? If *M* represents the norm, "the Hitler in us," aren't we protected by the recognition of inexorable human nature? Finally, if *M* is pushed in some mysterious manner by impenetrable supernatural forces, how can we resist them?

These three interpretations link up in neutralizing the past: When in *The Damned* Visconti makes Essenbeck's grandson a complete pervert, he opts for the symbol of *M* as the demented destroyer; when Syberberg constantly returns to the theme of "the Hitler in us," *M* becomes the implacable universal model; and in *The Ogre* as well as in *The Portage to San Cristóbal of A.H.,* the ogre—a good-natured version of *M*—and all that surrounds him, e.g., Hitler as the false Messiah predicted by the wise men, are only toys of occult forces that relieve man of all responsibility.

Besides, differing interpretations are often one and the same, even if at first they seem to contradict each other. Thus, *Lacombe Lucien,* for example, gives the impression that, human nature being what it is, a young lad of the times, no worse and no better than thousands of others, could become, *by chance,* collaborator or resistant (collaboration and resistance conveying the same image of death and abjectness since the film concludes with the information that "Lacombe Lucien was tried and executed. . . ."*

*The theme of chance and human nature represents a kind of leitmotiv in all literature tending to justify collaboration (although obviously the theme

Thus the first move is to take refuge behind destiny. But of all the interpretations of Nazi crimes, this one is the least easy to admit, and note that in a second shift the film quietly returns to the thesis of the irresponsible criminal: He is an idiot or demented. In fact, all the Gestapo auxiliaries in this film are clearly washouts and failures: Aubert, the failed bicycle champion; Tonin, the dismissed cop; Favre, the lunatic; Jean-Bernard des Voisins, the insipid dandy; not to mention the women and the Martiniquais. As for Lucien, is it accidental that he is shown as being brutal to animals, and on the whole as a person of limited intelligence? Evil and infamy are again limited to a small group the viewer can easily ignore. One may breathe again.

Distancing is taken even further in *The Ogre*. On the one hand, as Michel Tournier explains it, the entire chain of Nazi crimes is only the manifest expression of hidden forces,* and the book proposes to decipher the signs that would indicate something about these mysterious impulses—something that directly puts the crime outside the human condition. And when we are presented with a clearly criminal personality, he becomes isolated by an emphasis on his special characteristics, which puts him more in the demonic category than the human. Here is Blättchen, the SS officer in charge of racial studies at Kaltenborn: "With his tapering black goatee, big velvety eyes, inky serpentine brows and

---

of choice dominates resistance literature). (See Jacques Laurent's *Les Bêtises* as well as *Histoire égoïste*.)

*This is clearly stated in the foreword to the French original, not included, for some reason, in the American translation. Let us note in passing that this is exactly the thesis of Louis Pauwels and Jacques Bergier in *Le Matin des magiciens* (*The Morning of the Magicians*).

swarthy skull, this Mephisto in white overalls was an exceptionally pure specimen of the laboratory variety SS. . . ."[16]

None of those interpretations may be proved as correct or false; in fact we do not know. I have merely tried to show how each interpretation easily turns into a rationalization that normalizes, smoothes, and neutralizes our vision of the past. These voluntary or involuntary modalities of exorcism are those of today, but one need only turn toward the past to see among the Nazis themselves complex maneuvers to neutralize their own actions, a kind of exorcism accompanying the very course of the exterminations.

On October 4, 1943, Heinrich Himmler addressed the SS generals gathered in Posen (now Poznan, in Poland). Himmler speaks of the extermination of the Jewish people *(Die Ausrottung des judischen Volkes),* alluding to the terrible difficulties involved in such an action:

> Most of you know what it means to look at 100 corpses, 500 corpses, 1,000 corpses. Having borne that and nevertheless—some exceptional human weaknesses aside—having remained decent [*anständig geblieben zu sein*] has hardened us. This is a glorious, unwritten page of our history, one that will never be written. . . .

And here is the essential point:

> The wealth they [the Jews] had, we have taken. I gave strict orders—which SS Gruppenführer Pohl has carried out—that this wealth be promptly transferred to the

Reich. We have taken nothing. The few who have committed a crime will be punished according to the order
I gave at the beginning and which says: "Whoever takes
only one mark is liable for the death penalty." Several
members of the SS—and they are very few—have committed crimes. They will be sentenced to death without
mercy. We had the moral right, we had the duty to our
people to annihilate the people who wanted to annihilate us [*Wir hatten das moralische Recht, wir hatten die
Pflicht gegenüber unserem Volk, dieses Volk das uns
umbrigen wollte, umzubringen*]. But we do not have the
right to enrich ourselves, no matter if it were only a fur,
a watch, a mark, a cigarette, no matter what it might be.
While eliminating a germ, when all is said and done, we
do not wish to become infected by the germ and to die
from it. I will not allow the least zone of infestation to
form or to become established. Wherever it is formed,
we shall burn it out together [*werden wir sie gemeinsam
ausbrennen*]. Altogether, however, we can say that we
have accomplished the most difficult task for the love of
our people. And we have not sustained any damage to
our inner self, our soul and our character [*und wir haben
keinen Schaden in unserem Inneren, in unserer Seele, in
unserem Charakter daran genommen.*][17]

Quite openly, Himmler talks to his audience about
the annihilation of a people, an annihilation in which
some among them have taken part. He doesn't use any
circumlocution, doesn't camouflage the horror: 100
corpses, 500 corpses, 1,000 corpses . . . But at the same
time he undertakes the neutralization of what he is
going to say by linking the action he describes—the
extermination of the Jewish people—to stable values, to

rules everyone acknowledges, to the laws of everyday life. This "cover" has one clear aim: Insert extermination into the fabric of required behavior that is universally accepted, to evacuate its load of horror. The great virtues are first of all the accomplishment of a duty (imposed on the elite because it is an elite, etc.), a duty that is the foundation of morality. Secondly, the more specific obligation with respect to the defense of the race ("We had the moral right, we had the duty to our people to annihilate the people who wanted to annihilate us.") Then comes a transition to some of the strict rules of every organized society, notably Western bourgeois society: Don't steal; respect property under all circumstances, even if it is a tiny amount ("a mark, a cigarette . . ."). And following this, reference to the laws of personal, social, and racial hygiene ("While eliminating a germ, when all is said and done, we do not wish to become infected by the germ and to die from it"). Finally, a reaching out to great ideals: We have a soul and it is our duty to preserve it intact ("And we have not sustained any damage to our inner self . . ."). We belong to an elite who must accomplish the hardest labors, and, at the same time, keep to ourselves what we alone are fit to understand ("a glorious, unwritten page of our history, one that will never be written").

The yearning for destruction and death doesn't exclude shrinking from actual mass murder (Himmler's "faintheartedness" during his visit to extermination sites is well known). The "defenses" used by Himmler do not, therefore, contradict the gist of our whole interpretation. But one might point out another possible contradiction, a fault in the Himmlerian exorcism: If basic moral rules are enough to neutralize the fact of extermination, why insist on keeping it secret—not only for the duration of the war but forever? The answer seems simple to me: The rules are those of conventional morality, but the great mass of people, either because of incompetence or blindness, is not and never will be in a position to see the clear relationship between these rules and the extermination of the Jews. Like the prisoners in Plato's cave, the masses will never be able to turn and look at the light of truth without being blinded. Hence, the need for an elite, hence the speech to the SS generals.

Interpreted this way, Himmler's proposal is not without links to today's exorcism. For what is really at stake in one case and the other? To establish a barrier between the horror of the facts and the efforts, current or past (note in passing that the administrators of extermination used vague bureaucratic jargon—"final solution," "special action," "resettlement," etc.—to guard their secret and to make their own tasks easier), to insert the event into the banal course of everyday life; in short, to affirm that principles are maintained and respected, and that everything follows a normal course, according to laws dictated by necessity.

In *What Is Fascism?* Maurice Bardèche stresses that from the early Fifties on, the renaissance of fascism, and that of Nazism, carried an insupportable mortgage of committed crimes.[18] Ever since, when one evokes the renaissance of Nazism, of extreme anti-Semitism, of fascism, the memory of Auschwitz, that indelible reference point of the Western imagination, forms an obstacle impossible to evade. When systematic revisionism appeared in the Seventies, many people resorted somewhat to the other side of the same logic: The negation of Auschwitz opens the road to a return of fascism; in fighting revisionism, one fights against the revival of fascism. Here I have tried to develop a somewhat different argument.

If there has not been a revival of fascism (Nazism), it is because social, economic, and political conditions are entirely different from those Europe knew in the Twenties and Thirties. That said, the roads of the imaginary are mysterious, and at that level one can observe the revival of a certain attraction of Nazism, founded on the permanence of those elements whose nature I have tried to identify in the course of the first two chapters of this essay. And it is here that the exorcism of crimes intervenes. It is not revisionist manipulation of the facts which presents the danger of breaking the barrier of the imagination that is Auschwitz; that only makes up a minute aspect of the evolution we are perceiving. Much more significant is the progressive neutralization of this past as the generation directly involved gradually disappears and recollections fade. It is a neutralization in which we all take part, and which, as I have tried to indicate, began in a certain way at the heart of the Nazi phenomenon itself, even as the extermination was at its height. Blowing up the barrier is useless: It breaks up slowly under our eyes, sapped by the natural action of exorcism and evasion. And paralysis of language aside, what is the fundamental characteristic of this exorcism? To put the past back into bearable dimensions, superimpose it upon the known and respected progress of human behavior, put it in the identifiable course of things, into the unmysterious march of ordinary history, into the reassuring world of the rules that are the basis of our society—in short, into conformism and conformity.

One last aspect of this strange denial remains to be considered—a secondary aspect until now, but one whose eventual significance in the evolution of phantasms and of attitudes toward the past and toward the future is significant. And that is the transformation of the image of the Jew.

It is no sign of undue obsession to see in this theme a facet of the changes that concern us. Relations with the Jews became in the Nazi era a point of rupture where ordinary behavior no longer held. Since then, it has become the symbolic problem that sums up the most striking side of this past, and it is indeed where one has to look for some expressions of a modification in the unstable equilibrium that has established itself in the imagination of our societies since the war. (I will discuss here neither garden-variety anti-Semitism nor the political debates that can influence this subject. The field of inquiry remains the same as for this essay as a whole: the new discourse and its possible connections with the past.) Within limits, this last facet of exorcism is an inversion of signs and the beginning of a new discourse about Evil.*

*I should repeat that the texts analyzed here do not reflect in any way upon the *intentions* of their authors. It goes without saying that George Steiner, who is greatly conscious of his Jewishness and to whom we owe some overwhelming pages on the Holocaust (Lieber's monologue in *The Portage to San Cristóbal of A.H.* is especially moving), does not voluntarily invert the signs concerning the Jews. Nevertheless, the texts carry their own logic and their inevitable echoes. Hitler's speech, which Steiner leaves with-

Erster Punkt. Article one. Because you must understand that I did not invent. It was not Adolf Hitler who dreamt up the master race. Who conceived of enslaving inferior peoples. Lies. Lies. It was in the doss house, in the *Männerheim* that I first understood. . . . God help me, but that was long ago. And the lice. Large as a thumbnail. 1910, 1911. What does it matter now? It was there that I first understood your secret power. The secret power of your teaching. Of *yours.* A chosen people.

This is the beginning of Adolf Hitler's speech about the Jews in *The Portage to San Cristóbal of A.H.*[19] And in *Hitler, a Film from Germany,* Syberberg, too, imagines Hitler's final speech:

> I believe and avow, at least once, seriously what it was really all about, my struggle, *Mein Kampf,* the program of our final goal. . . . We learned from the practice of the Jewish people how religious racial purity and a sense of mission by a chosen people can help us achieve world dominion.
>
> Thinking of Jerusalem for two thousand years. In every prayer, every day, until they won. My respects. We may be small, but once a man stood up in Galilee, and today his teachings govern the entire world, for that is what we learn from the Jewish who from now on will have nothing more to do with Moses, the Egyptian prince, or Jesus. . . .
>
> Strength does not lie in the majority . . . it lies in the purity of the willingness to offer sacrifices, and that means the eradication—and I say this now, consistently

out an answer, will seem to many readers to embody the essential purport of the novel.

and logically, ruthlessly—the extermination of the divine people through the natural superiority . . . of the chosen racial elite of the Aryans. . . .[20]

Here is a new discourse about the Jews, in both instances with Hitler as the mouthpiece. But before we return to these texts, a reminder is in order about the archetypical Jew in the other works under discussion here.

In some cases, it is his absence that is so striking. It has been noted more than once how in his memoirs Speer avoided the Jewish problem in general and that of the extermination in particular,* which, in all logic, he could not ignore. We have also noted the semidisappearance of the final solution in Joachim Fest's *Hitler, a Career,* the film based on his Hitler biography. As for *Lili Marleen,* the extermination is reduced to those mysterious snapshots that pass from one hand to another and find refuge for a brief instant between the breasts of the beautiful Willie.

A doubtful Jew appears in *Lacombe Lucien;* a weak and ungrateful one in Christian de La Mazière's *The Captive Dreamer.* At best they are there only as ectoplasm. More significant still is the return, in several of the works central to this discussion, of the theme of the triumphant Jew.

Take, for example, the glory of the Mendelsohns in *Lili Marleen:* they are the only ones to emerge from the war physically and morally unscathed, the only win-

---

*Various sources give the impression that Speer knew more about the final solution than he was willing to admit and that he was less discreet about the Jewish problem than his memoirs would have one believe. See Mathias Schmitt, *op. cit.*

ners in a ruined Europe where millions have died; where the singer Willie, the symbol of a naïve and faithful people, has been sent out into the night; and where even the Nazi power has been destroyed. Only the rule of the Mendelsohn clan and money remains. Rainer Werner Fassbinder had already done an early sketch of the "rich Jew" in his *Shadow of Angels,* where the prostitute, Lili Brest, asks the "rich Jew" to strangle her. There too, single people are shown crushed by modern life, power, and money. In *Shadow of Angels,* the Jew's success is both more striking and more ambiguous than in *Lili Marleen.* He dominates the town because he knows how to manipulate the levers of power, but he is only a vulgar businessman, a swindler, who in other respects seems prey to anguish and doubt. There is nothing here of the total assurance, the patrician pride, the all-powerfulness of a Mendelsohn—who in the final scene of *Lili Marleen* is not shown among the others, but is framed, as in a portrait, an exemplary and mythic personage incarnating, with a smile on his lips, the quintessence of power.

The "rich Jew" and the patriarch Mendelsohn are well-known people, but perhaps their power and their money guard the secret they have gathered around them. The rich Jew reigns over his world, over property and hoodlums, but suddenly it becomes clear that he is also in league with the police and the town's notables. His enormous black limousine surges out of darkness and disappears into the night. As for the patriarch Mendelsohn, he knows how to pull all the strings from behind the scenes. He blocks Lili's return to Switzerland. He sends his emissaries into the heart of Nazi Germany to snatch his son. He is like a spider sitting in the center of his web, but a spider whose repugnant aspect would have disappeared. A master of lies and duplicity, he seems a symbol of detachment and nobility.

In *The Ogre,* the triumph of the Jewish world partakes of the superhuman. For it is Ephraim, the fragile Jewish child, who in the final scene emerges as the supernatural force. Nazism has been destroyed. Everything is in flames and ruins. Tiffauges, the carrier of the child, is swallowed in a marsh, inexplicably thrown down by a superhuman weight.

> He tried to stop and turn back, but an irresistible force bore down on his shoulders. The deeper his feet sank into the waterlogged swamp, the more he felt the boy—so thin and diaphanous—weighing down on him like a lump of lead. On he went, and still the mud rose around his legs, and the load that was crushing him grew heavier with every step.
>
> He had to make a superhuman effort now to overcome the viscous resistance grinding in his belly and breast, but he persevered, knowing all was as it should be. When he turned to look up for the last time at Ephraim, all he saw was a six-pointed star turning slowly against the black sky.[21]

But on the whole these are only reflections of quite ordinary themes. More unusual is the language George Steiner gives to Hitler—a Hitler his captors already consider a Jew.*

*Note in passing that this "insinuation" about Hitler's Jewishness was spread at the beginning of the Nazi movement. Hitler's nephew exploited it to make money. Hans Frank, the ex–governor general of Poland, picked it up

To conquer its promised land, to cut down or lay in bondage all who stand in its path, to proclaim itself eternal. . . . To slaughter a city because of an idea, because of a vexation over words. Oh that was a high invention, a device to alter the human soul. Your invention. One Israel, one *Volk,* one leader. Moses, Joshua, the anointed king who has slain his thousands, no his ten-thousands, and dances before the ark. . . ."[22]

The argument Hitler develops in this book and that no one answers is simple: Jewish fanaticism, which rests on the assurance of being the chosen people, a unique conception in antiquity, gave birth to a tide that finally led to another chosen race, the Nazis. In a natural reaction and proper reversal, they turn against the Jews and destroy them. The world has room for only one chosen people. The argument, however, is divided in two: Jewish fanaticism taught the Nazis fanaticism and destruction; as for the other face of Judaism (the universalism of the Ten Commandments, and of Jesus and Marx), it could only attract Hitler's hatred and call for extermination.

Next, Hitler defends himself against the charge of enormous crimes. Did not Stalin and his system, at first supported by the Jews, exterminate on just as large a scale? Finally, in a strange peroration of this strange speech, Hitler tells his kidnappers become his judges: "You owe your state to me. Without 'the Holocaust' there would have been no Israel." And, a final point,

at Nürnberg for reasons never satisfactorily explained. Some historians took it up again in the Fifties. The idea is interesting as a measure of how much Hitler may have been obsessed by it. Today the rumor is considered plain gossip without plausible foundation.

this unjust Israel that inflicts suffering on those around it, could it not be the consequence, the reflection—perhaps the imitation?—of that shameful past?

> It was the Holocaust that gave you the courage of injustice, that made you drive the Arab out of his home, out of his field, because he was lice-eaten and without resource, because he was in your divinely ordered way. That made you endure knowing that those whom you had driven out were rotting in refugee camps not ten miles away, buried alive in despair and lunatic dreams of vengeance. Perhaps I *am* the Messiah, the true Messiah, the new Sabbatai whose infamous deeds were allowed by God in order to bring His people home.[23]

Steiner's story—be it as a book or play—has caused some kind of scandal. I shall not repeat the arguments used on both sides, nor will I return to a discussion of the fictionalization or the aesthetization of Nazism. Our problem is the inversion of signs and the *apparent* identification of the author with some of A.H.'s arguments. George Steiner himself, retorting to an attack by Martin Gilbert, has answered this charge in two ways:

> To this day, readers wonder whether Milton is, finally, "of Satan's party"; to this day, we remain in anguish over the fact that Dostoevsky provides no answer to the overwhelming cynicism of the Grand Inquisitor in *The Brothers Karamazov*. It is just this wonder, this anguish, which constitutes the impact and freedom of a literary text. . . .

Further on, Steiner adds:

The answers to "A.H." *must* come from the audience, from the readers, from each and every one of those whose moral being is implicated in the continuing bestialities of the twentieth century. The relation between writer and audience is one of trust, it is, in Sartre's phrase, "a pact of generosity . . ."[24]

Steiner's arguments cannot be answered on a purely abstract level. He refers to Milton and to Dostoevsky, and he could add Lautréamont and Baudelaire, the Marquis de Sade and the Book of Job, as well as countless other names and titles. Still, the answer doesn't convince, for two reasons.

Assuming the basic idea that George Steiner wanted to convey was that of the necessary link, the necessary cosmic symbiosis, between Good and Evil, then why, as Hyam Maccoby pointed out, did Steiner feel it compelling to prove his point in such a way? "It seems to be the *reductio ad absurdum* of Steiner's theory of culture that this polymath, dedicated humanist, and apostle of ideas should have felt it necessary to dignify Hitler by elevating him into a metaphysical principle."[25]

The answer doesn't convince on another count: We deal with the "here and now," with issues laden with concrete emotion and existing prejudice, with themes that in our very midst easily feed attitudes and actions, too. The "pact of generosity" between reader and writer assumes some sharing of knowledge and some community of values; very often this is not the case. And eloquence—the real eloquence of the pseudo-Hitler—may reach deeply into those murky labyrinths of present-day fantasies about Nazism or the Jews, the fantasies that are the stuff this essay is made of.

And so it is that in the face of the essential aspects of Nazism, there are not only willful denials but also and mainly inadequacy of our modes of expression and interpretation, which is easily turned into defenses against the very impact of the past. Thus exorcism, in all possible meanings of the word.

4

"When I think of Hitler, nothing comes to mind," Karl Kraus wrote at the time of the rise of Nazism. He was often reproached for this statement, but Kraus may have seen the situation more clearly than Brecht, who for a long time believed in the power of ridicule. One remembers the slogan "Laugh of the beast."

In facing this past today, we have come back to words, to images, to phantasms. They billow in serried waves, sometimes covering the black rock that one sees from all sides off the shores of our common history. For the contemporary imagination, Nazism has become one of the supreme metaphors, that of Evil. It is nourished by memory, by scientific inquiry, and by numerous everyday references, by literature, by art. And nevertheless its expression, taken as a whole, leaves a strange impression of insufficiency, which the new discourse has come to correct in its own way, creating a malaise both because of what it says and doesn't say. One feels, here and there, the return of a fascination.

The paralysis of language faced with certain aspects of Nazism has been demonstrated in the preceding chapter, as well as the apparent impossibility of arriving, by purely literary reevocation, at a penetration to the core of the phenomenon. A few words still need to be said here about the problems of rational and scientific explanation, notably in the writing of its history.

Confronted by what seems to me to be the essential character of Nazism, its psychological dimension, historical inquiry seems to strike at an irreducible anomaly.* The emotional hold Hitler and his movement maintained on many Germans to the bitter end, and well beyond the frontiers of the Reich, the spell it wove for so many people, the actual mutation of behavior it set off, defies all customary interpretation and can never be explained coherently within the framework of a historiography in which political, social, or economic explanations predominate. The constant preoccupation with Nazism since the end of World War II and the resurgence of phantasms on the subject of Hitlerism no doubt raise the same problem. The manifest presence of this unknown determinant has changed nothing about the routine of research. It is true that the psychohistorical investigation of Nazism has become a discipline in itself—which seems to answer the objection. But it must be admitted that this approach has proved disappointing because of an excessively schematic application of

*In the sense used by Thomas Kuhn in *The Structure of Scientific Revolutions* (Chicago: University of Chicago Press, 1970).

concepts both too general and too worn out: At best it seems artificial. (My own study of Nazi anti-Semitism poses the same problems.)

Remember Speer and all the others. Or these few lines from Bullock's biography:

> Hitler's power to bewitch an audience has been likened to the occult arts of the African medicine man . . . ; others have compared it to the sensitivity of a medium and the magnetism of a hypnotist. . . . The former French ambassador speaks of him as "a man possessed"; Hermann Rauschning writes: "Dostoevsky might well have invented him, with the morbid derangement and the pseudo-creativeness of his hysteria"; one of the Defense Counsel at the Nuremberg trials, Dr. Dix, quoted a passage from Goethe's *Dichtung und Wahrheit* describing the Demoniac and applied this very aptly to Hitler. With Hitler, indeed, one is uncomfortably aware of never being far from the realm of the irrational."[1]

For an Oxford historian to express himself like that, there has to have been overwhelming evidence. Ever since, despite a mass of research of all kinds, we have not advanced much.

The uncanny hold Hitler had over people, the frenzy of the crowds, the persecution and extermination of the Jews eliminate in fact the possibility of any overall explanation.* Thus the theory of fascism collapses when

---

*The following pages will take up again an argument developed several years ago in "L'Extermination des Juifs d'Europe: pour une étude historique globale" ("The Extermination of Europe's Jews: Toward a Global Historic Study"), *Revue d'études juives,* CXXXV, vols. 1–3, January–September 1976, p. 113ff., and, more recently, in my "De l'Antisemitiance è l'Extermination: Un Essai d'historiographie," *Le Débet,* September 1982.

faced with the specificity of Hitler's anti-Semitism. It is certainly possible to allege that the centrality accorded to Nazi anti-Judaism is a "Jewish interpretation . . . based on the most appalling of all human experiences,"[2] and can in fact be explained as an aspect of what the various fascist movements have in common—namely, anti-Marxism. One need not be Jewish to realize that Jews, not Marxists, were the target of Hitler's first and last declarations (the letter to Gemlich in 1919 and the last words of his political testament in April 1945); or to see the obvious centrality of the anti-Jewish theme in the recent collection of Hitler's writings in the first part of his career;[3] or to admit the importance of Martin Bormann's remark, made in 1944 in Hitler's presence (and Bormann was the most faithful echo of his master's voice), "National Socialist doctrine is totally anti-Jewish, which means anti-communist and anti-Christian. All that is part of National Socialism and all of it contributes to the battle against Judaism."[4] Is there anything similar, for example, in Italian fascism?

The "totalitarian" explanation runs into the same obstacles. According to the theory of totalitarianism, the elite of the system does not have faith in its own ideology. Thus the higher up one moves in the hierarchy, the less one believes in the reality of the "enemy," who becomes merely a functional element in the system of domination.

"The Jews were murdered," Horkheimer and Adorno write, "at a time when the fascist chieftains [*fascist* is the equivalent of *totalitarian* in the present context] could have replaced the anti-Semitic points of their program . . . as easily as teams of workers can be transferred from one assembly line to another. . . ."[5]

This is a statement without any connection to the reality of national socialism. In the Nazi system, the higher one rose in the hierarchy, the greater one's faith in the ideology. That was certainly true of the supreme leader. According to a common interpretation of totalitarianism, enemies are fought and persecuted in order to galvanize energies and to paralyze all possible opposition. Mostly the people are informed about the persecution of enemies, no matter what form that persecution takes. The Nazis themselves didn't keep quiet about the execution of the SA chieftains or their other political "opponents." But one knows that the attitude toward the Jews was not the same. At the time of the final phase—that of massive extermination—the impossible was attempted in order to hide the facts. In Nazi eyes, the extermination of the Jews was a vital necessity. It represented a sacred mission. This was neither a gesture to set an example nor a means to attain other ends.

Marxist historians look for an explanation in the alleged economic role of the Jews. They forget that the persecution and massacre of Europe's Jews did away with a sizable work force at a time when the Nazi Reich was engaged in the most desperate phases of total war. At the culmination of hostilities, less than a quarter of the Jews in each convoy escaped extermination upon arrival at the camp. And those, according to all the evidence, were only temporarily spared and allowed to die of exhaustion. According to the statistics, the final solution was a loss to the German war economy for which the wealth taken from the victims was no compensation.

But here again Nazi sources speak for themselves.

123

When in 1941 Reichskommissar H. Lohse asked Alfred Rosenberg if it was necessary to exterminate all the Jews in the East "without taking economic interests into consideration, Wehrmacht needs for skilled workers in the arms industry, for example," the minister told him: "In principle, no economic consideration whatever will be taken into account in the solution of this problem."*

The "narrow" economic explanation must not be confused with an effort at a much broader Marxist theory, basing racial anti-Semitism and, by extension, the final solution on the hostility of some social strata toward the "class" the Jews represented within the context of the crisis of capitalism. As Abram Leon writes in *The Jewish Question: A Marxist Interpretation,*

> Historically, the success of racism means that capitalism has managed to channel the anti-capitalist consciousness of the masses into a form that antedates capitalism and which no longer exists except in a vestigial state; this vestige [the commercial and financial functions of Jews during the pre-capitalist era and during the rise of modern capitalism] is nevertheless still sufficiently great to give a certain appearance of reality to the myth.[6]

Abram Leon caught a glimpse of the paradoxical nature of this explanation and attempted to reply:

---

*Nürnberg Documents PS-3666. It has been shown that in some circumstances the economic imperatives seemed to have priority over the imperative of extermination. On at least two occasions even Hitler gave the order to postpone the execution of some Jews for economic reasons. But such cases remained exceptions. No documentary proof allows the conclusion that at any time—except for the last months of the war—was exploitation of Jewish slave labor considered more important than the extermination of the Jews.

The irony of history wills that the most radical anti-Semitic ideology in all history should triumph precisely in the period when Judaism is on the road of economic and social assimilation. But like all "ironies of history" this seeming paradox is very understandable. At the time when the Jew represented "capital," he was indispensable to society. There could be no question of destroying him. At the present time, capitalist society, on the edge of the abyss, tries to save itself by resurrecting the Jew and the hatred of the Jews. . . .⁷*

But such an interpretation does not say how racist hatred based on socioeconomic antagonism—which on other occasions led to plunder, expulsion, slavery, or sporadic killing (for example in the colonies)—here results in a fierce desire for total extermination; it explains even less why the theme of the "capitalist Jew" had been of secondary importance in the Nazi mythology compared to the "revolutionary Jew." (And wasn't Hitler's first book, written in collaboration with Dietrich Eckart, *Der Bolschewismus von Moses bis Lenin* [*Bolshevism from Moses to Lenin*]?)

Behind the inertia of the interpretations, it is the inertia of the basic postulates that manifests itself. Nazism remains a constant stumbling block for Marxist historiography. One can explain the formation of the movement in social terms, the Nazi accession to power in terms of economic interests, Nazi politics until around 1936 within the same parameters. But afterward nothing seems to respond anymore to this scheme of analysis,

*It should be stressed that Abram Leon finished his work in 1943, thus his knowledge of events could only be incomplete. (He died two years later at Auschwitz.)

and if one wants to maintain it, it is necessary to eliminate the central role of Adolf Hitler; the foundations and the stages of his racial policy; his war in the West, especially his declaration of war on the United States; and finally his policy of exterminating the Jews. In sum, what's left is a Nazism without Nazism, an image of events where it is difficult to distinguish between a Hitler and a Roosevelt, and to separate Nazi racial policies from the most banal manifestation of the class struggle. That is normalization to excess in the name of a preestablished conceptual framework.

The revisionist far right holds to the same objective. Among Marxists the "final solution" remains marginal and almost nonexistent when compared to the general explanation. For the revisionist, the final solution is factually very uncertain, or, more simply, it just never happened. Add to that the malaise of liberal historians dealing with such an oddity in a context where everything should be accessible to rational analysis, and one ends up with a concept at once abstract and "cleaned up," such as we have already discussed—or with such parodies as *Hitler, a Career.* *

The liberal position is often identified with a "totalitarian" conception of Nazism, allowing the stark contrast between free governments and an indistinct totalitarian monster in which Nazism and Stalinism are joined together within the framework of the same mechanism of domination. A vague theory, which once again spirits away the essential nature of Nazism. But beyond

---

*The present-day controversy between "intentionalists" and "fuctionalists" is significant at the level of "decision-making analysis" but can add nothing to the overall historiographical interpretation.

the totalitarian paradigm, another implicit model appears, one that found its implicit formulation in Joachim Fest's biography. It can be summarized as follows: Hitler was not an anomaly, and Nazism as a whole was not either; whatever the horror of certain aspects of the regime, they were, after all, only manifestations pushed to the extreme of tendencies of the time, of attitudes of the West toward the Jews, among other things. As Hitler puts it in Syberberg's film, addressing Germans, Europeans, everyone: "I am the expression of your most secret desires." Thus there is an osmosis between Hitler and his time; Nazism is not a reflection but rather a precipitate of the tendencies of that time. This is necessarily true, in a way, but too general to allow an interpretation.

And finally this remains—and here we are back in the middle of the new discourse: For Michel Tournier, as for Pauwels and Bergier, the comprehension of Nazism passes through the mystical, through a deciphering of supernatural forces, the key to which is not given to us. For George Steiner, too, it is less a matter of the Hitler phenomenon as such but of Hitler as the false Messiah who could annihilate creation. The cosmic view of Hans-Jürgen Syberberg leaves the same impression. If that is so, all rational action within the order of politics becomes ridiculous.* One doesn't fight against the antichrist or a false Messiah by using the full powers of-

---

*The same argument is well expressed in Leon Wieseltier's review of Syberberg's movie: "The objection to Syberberg's mysticism could be put this way: that it offers no basis from which Hitler could have been resisted in his time. . . . The view that Hitler was inevitable, that what engendered him was destiny, is essentially a dismissal of politics. Why resist salvation? Messiahs batten on this selfish desire to believe. . . ." (Leon Wieseltier, "Syberberg's Hitler," *New Republic,* 8 March 1980.)

fered by such and such an article of a constitution. Joachim Fest's historical fatalism finally comes back to the same thing: If Nazism was the necessary response to the problems of the time, there is nothing for the individual to do but silently submit to the flux of the spirit of the times, the blind movement of a Hegelian or Spenglerian *Weltgeist* carrying away, in an irresistible rush and without recourse, individual will and rational perception.

That implies, in fact, an implicit or explicit belief in a secret order of things determining the apparent course of events; it is thus a matter of a complete devaluation of the order of politics, and of the replacement of the economic determinism of the Marxists by a determinism more mysterious but no less real.

And here we are also confronted by a moral dilemma: If reason is impotent and if events depend on mysterious and incomprehensible rules, crimes cannot be judged according to our conventional criteria. Hence the grotesque character, in George Steiner's novel, of the West German government's juridical preoccupations in facing the eventuality of Hitler's return. Hence also, in the same work, the ambiguous character of the final trial. Hence, finally, Joachim Fest's distinction between moral responsibility and historical grandeur.

And thus one perceives in the new discourse, or at least in certain of its most striking works, beneath the proposed interpretations, a kind of empty place where there is room neither for the rational interpretation of events nor for free and effective political action, nor for moral and legal responsibility in the usual meaning of the term. And if we reject, because of its simplicity, the

Marxist interpretation of Nazism, and that of the revisionists because of its openly lying character, we discover, faced with Hitlerism, within the framework of a new discourse that easily encompasses positions that are apparently more classical, the failure of our ideologies and the impotence of our traditional approaches.

What remains, therefore, are those attempts at reelaboration and reevocation that characterize the new discourse. Their defenders have seen in it a reestablishment of the truth, a necessary exploration, a salutary warning; their critics a nostalgia that dare not say its name. "Fascism is not only an event of yesterday," Liliana Cavani writes, apropos of her film *The Night Porter:*

> It is with us still, here and elsewhere. As dreams do, my film brings back to the surface a repressed "history"; today this past is still deep within us. . . . What interested me was to explore this cellar of the present, to inquire into the human subconscious; it was to offer up that which troubles me in order to trouble others so that all of us can live wakefully. It was to stimulate, to give a point of departure for understanding why the fascists are again among us—not the old ones, the nostalgics who are, one might say, caricatures, but the new ones, the young antidemocrats of my generation.[8]

And, as counterpoint, Marie Chaix:

> This spreading nostalgia is becoming nauseating. . . . When Lacombe Lucien chews a blade of grass in a pleasant meadow, his eyes gliding over the beautiful body of "the little Jewess," or when a Nazi officer (who

twelve years later will become the seductive Night Porter) leans, lips trembling, toward the wound of his victim to kiss her blood, I want to vomit. . . . The memories of those who are fascinated by Nazism and the Occupation are much too short. . . . All of you who dress in the fashionable Occupation style, who are fascinated by the Nazis, who are lulled by the tune of "Maréchal nous voilà [*Marshal, We are There*]" are unwilling to acknowledge that tomorrow it could all begin again. Everything is prepared for it, and there is therefore something to be feared about this poisoned flowering, which with its kitsch tinsel strains to absolve one of the most frightful horrors of history. . . .[9]

I think I have shown in the course of the preceding pages that the new discourse on Nazism, voluntary or not, has not only often fed a new fascination for this past but has also helped us to understand something about the mechanism of this attraction. That leaves unanswered the essential question, that of the general foundations of this hold. Let me propose, in these last pages, a few very sketchy remarks. They are not meant to be an answer to the questions asked here, but, at most, to hint at possible approaches and call for more systematic inquiry.

Let us take first the contradictory elements unveiled by the analysis of the images and of the texts: the value put on the order of things as they are, on the one hand, and on death and destruction on the other.

On the side of the affirmation of order, the kitsch vision reinforces the aesthetic criteria of a submissive mass, serene in its quest for harmony, always partial to sentimentality. The view of Hitler as Everyman fits perfectly into this tranquil perspective; thus the Führer is close to the world of homely cottages and to everyone's heart.

But facing the kitsch aesthetic is the unfathomable world of myths; facing the visions of harmony, the lights of the apocalypse; facing the young girls crowned with flowers and the snow-capped peaks of the Bavarian Alps, the call to the dead of the Feldherrnhalle, the ecstasy of the Götterdämmerung, the visions of the end of the world. Facing Hitler as Everyman—the fondler of blond children and fancier of adventure films and cream tarts—a blind force thrown toward nothingness, butcher hooks, and visions of cities going up in flames. Facing the tranquil force of moral values is the flickering light of the fires of extermination.

In this contradictory series, it is not one thing or another that is decisive by itself; it is their coexistence that gives the totality its significance.

In his *Uranus*, Marcel Aymé describes the execution of some collaborationist militiamen and its observation through the window of their dining room by a couple who are sympathizers of the victims: "The sight of those two cautious, dismal and mean-spirited specimens of the petty bourgeoisie eyeing the victims from their Renaissance dining-room and titillating each other and jigging up and down in the folds of the curtains, just like dogs . . .* Georges Bataille, who quotes this passage in his *Death and Sensuality,* sees in it an example of the accord between erotic play and the spectacle of violence and death, but under the circumstances the framework

---

*Cited in Georges Bataille, *Death and Sensuality* (New York: Walker & Co., 1962), p. 107.

also plays a decisive role: It is there to protect them, to assure them of their normality, and to allow them to have their orgasm in the sight of violence and death.

"All the frantic gaiety that greeted [Hitler's arrival] came from a perspective of nothingness which each individual proclaimed for himself, in celebration of pure nihilism." This is true, but only with a necessary support system: well-polished floors, well-upholstered armchairs, and a piano in the drawing room with a Mozart score placed on the music stand between two candlesticks where everybody can see it.

Does all this raise again the usual categories of sadomasochism, of the "authoritarian personality," or the clinical-historical hypotheses of Reich, Fromm, or Adorno?

Nothing of the sort. Once again it is a matter here of the convergence of two series of themes, of images, of emotions, of phantasms that cut across a culture and a society. One can, in this convergence, recognize a terrain favorable for the nurturing of certain personal tendencies, but there is no causal connection nor any delimited psychological determinism there.

In his analysis of *The Cabinet of Dr. Caligari,* Siegfried Kracauer illuminates the constant oscillation in Robert Wiene's film between tyranny and chaos, a theme, according to Kracauer, that reflects the profound malaise of "the collective [German] soul."[10] The horror of tyranny pushes toward chaos, fear of chaos brings back tyranny without any victory of the one over the other, and hence comes an adulation of the existing order and, *at the same time,* a yearning for chaos, for destruction, for death.

132

In evoking the great ceremonial occasions of the party, Joachim Fest writes:

> The resort to ceremonials also reveals a strenuous desire to stylize, to represent the triumph of order over a shifting existence [that of Hitler] forever threatened by chaos. We might call these efforts techniques of exorcism undertaken by a terrified mind. When certain contemporaries likened all the to-do with marching columns, forests of banners and blocks of humanity to the rites of primitive tribes, the comparison was not so artificial as it sounded.[11]

But there again the displacement of one tendency by another bends the image. It is only the constant interaction of the two impulses that made of Nazism a new synthesis and gave it its mysterious, hypnotic power.

At the level of the daily practice of murder, the sterilization of language, the demand for order and for the permanence of ordinary norms no doubt serve as defense and protection. But at the same time, apocalyptic reverie creates a general atmosphere and vehicle for phantasms of slavery and extermination. It is this balance of general visions and precise defenses—onto which the most complex individual obsessions can be grafted—that pushes ahead and protects at the same time. In the extermination of the Jews in particular, these two fundamental and contradictory themes of the Nazi imagination find their expression and their satisfaction. For if you eliminate contagion, bacteria, and infection, isn't that a return to natural harmony and order through absolute purification? And to engage in combat against the very incarnation of Evil, the principle of darkness that threatens mankind with the most terrible of slaveries, isn't that to throw oneself into a supreme enterprise that will result either in final salvation or ultimate destruction? According to *Mein Kampf*, if the Jew triumphs, his diadem will be the funerary crown of mankind, and a world newly emptied of human beings will roll through space. Triumph or the eventuality of an irremediable catastrophe are equally possible.

The call for a universal conflagration, often issued by religious or secular millennial sects in the past as well as today,* never goes hand in hand with a submission to existing order. If often—in the West as in the East, in the North as in the South of the planet—peoples have venerated oppressive, barbarous, and terrorist power, and sometimes an exterminating one as under Stalin, *they have never at one and the same time venerated oppression and propagated apocalyptic visions.* "The morrows that sing" was not a metaphor for the end of time. Until now, organized societies or stable power structures were never attracted to apocalypse, only terrified by the prospect of it. This is where the difference from Nazism stands out.

Nazi power, in the duality we have tried to analyze, was the expression, singular up to now, of a flow of ideas, emotions, and phantasms that are kept separate in all other modern Western societies.

*On this subject, see Norman Cohn's excellent book *The Pursuit of the Millennium*, rev. ed. (New York: Oxford, 1970). For a more recent study, see James Rhodes, *The Hitler Movement: A Modern Millenarian Revolution* (Stanford: Stanford University Press, 1980).

No doubt Nazism in its singularity, as in its general aspects, is the result of a large number of social, economic, and political factors, of the coming to a head of frequently analyzed ideological currents, and of the meeting of the most archaic myths and the most modern means of terror. All that is known today. Moreover, it is evident that the reappearance of movements similar to Nazism—whatever the precise form—depends above all on social and political conditions, at once multiple and convergent, that one does not perceive on the horizon, but that leaves unanswered the question of the context of the imponderable elements, the fusion of opposites that I have tried to illuminate.

Now, this fusion is only the expression of a kind of malaise in civilization, linked to the acceptance of civilization, but also to its fundamental rejection. *Modern society and the bourgeois order are perceived both as an accomplishment and as an unbearable yoke. Hence this constant coming and going between the need for submission and the reveries of total destruction, between love of harmony and the phantasms of apocalypse, between the enchantment of Good Friday and the twilight of the gods.* Submission nourishes fury, fury clears its conscience in the submission. To these opposing needs, Nazism—in the constant duality of its representations—offers an outlet; in fact, Nazism found itself to be the expression of these opposing needs. Today these aspirations are still there, and their reflections in the imaginary as well.

But this duality is grafted onto a much more profound contradiction made up of a dream of all-powerfulness and the accepted risk of annihilation. This is certainly part of the romantic tradition, but above all it is a vision that, better perhaps than the liberal or Marxist vision, explains the profound conflict of man facing modernity. The liberal creed and the Marxist creed imply assurance of salvation by the cumulative acquisition of knowledge and power. Neither liberalism nor Marxism responds to man's archaic fear of the transgression of some limits of knowledge and power (you shall not eat the fruit . . .), thus hiding what remains the fundamental temptation: the aspiration for total power, which, by definition, is the supreme transgression, the ultimate challenge, the superhuman combat that can be settled only by death.

Linked as it is to a great extent to the rise of modernity, does this vision still run through our imagination, does it remain a temptation for today and for tomorrow? We know that the dream of total power is always present, though dammed up, repressed by the Law. Also constant is the temptation to break the Law, even at the risk of destruction. With this difference—which perhaps tempers, or on the contrary exacerbates, the apocalyptic dreams: This time, to reach for total power is to assure oneself, and all of mankind as well, of being engulfed in total and irremediable destruction.

Notes

INTRODUCTION

1. Albert Speer, *Spandau: The Secret Diaries,* translated by Richard and Clara Winston (New York: Macmillan, 1976), p. 114.

2. Nigel Andrews, "Hitler as Entertainment," *American Film,* April 1978, p. 53.

3. Susan Sontag, "Syberberg's Hitler," in *Under the Sign of Saturn* (New York: Farrar, Straus & Giroux, 1980), p. 164.

CHAPTER 1

1. Abraham Moles, *Psychologie du kitsch. L'art du bonheur (Psychology of Kitsch. The Art of Happiness)* (Paris: Denoël, 1971), pp. 19–20.

2. Albert Speer, *Inside the Third Reich,* translated by Richard and Clara Winston (New York: Macmillan, 1970), p. 162.

3. Jacques Laurent, *Histoire égoïste* (Paris: La Table Ronde, 1976), p. 174.

4. Marguerite Yourcenar, *Coup de grâce,* translated by Grace Frick in collaboration with the author (New York: Farrar, Straus & Giroux, 1957), p. 125.

5. Michel Tournier, *The Ogre* (New York: Doubleday, 1972), pp. 283–84.

6. Christian de La Mazière, *The Captive Dreamer,* translated by Francis Stuart (New York: Saturday Review Press/E. P. Dutton, 1974), p. 31.

7. Ibid., p. 92.

8. Yourcenar, *Coup de grâce*.

9. La Mazière, op. cit.

10. Pierre Cadars and Francis Courtade, *Le Cinéma nazi* (Paris: Losfeld, 1972), p. 41.

11. Hans-Jürgen Syberberg, *Hitler, a Film from Germany,* translated by Joachim Neugroschel (New York: Farrar, Straus & Giroux, 1982), p. 61.

12. Ibid., pp. 155–56.

13. Sontag, "Fascinating Fascism," in *Under the Sign of Saturn,* p. 90.

14. J. P. Stern, letter to the editor, *New York Review of Books,* 29 May 1980.

15. Joachim Fest, *Hitler* (Berlin: Ullstein Verlag, pp. 699–700).

16. Tournier, *The Ogre,* p. 368.

17. Cadars and Courtade, *Le Cinéma nazi,* p. 44.

18. Michel Tournier, *Le Vent Paraclet* (Paris: Gallimard, 1977), p. 183.

19. Syberberg, *Hitler, a Film from Germany,* p. 9.

CHAPTER 2

1. Jean Tulard, *Napoléon ou le mythe du sauveur (Napoleon or the Myth of the Savior)* (Paris: Fayard, 1977), p. 597.

2. Albert Speer, *Infiltration* (New York: Macmillan, 1981).

3. Albert Speer, *Inside the Third Reich* (London: Weidenfeld, 1970), p. 317.

4. Speer, *Inside the Third Reich,* trans. by Richard and Clara Winston (New York: Macmillan, 1970), pp. 488–89.

5. Werner Maser, *Adolf Hitler: Legende, Mythos, Wirklichkeit* (Munich: Bechtle, 1971), p. 9.

6. George Steiner, *The Portage to San Cristóbal of A.H.* (New York: Simon & Schuster, 1981).

7. Ibid., p. 72.

8. Syberberg, *Hitler, a Film from Germany*, p. 151.

9. Speer, *Inside the Third Reich*, p. 131.

10. Ibid., p. 132.

11. Ibid., p. 171.

12. Ibid, pp. 479–80.

13. Joachim Fest, *Hitler*, translated by Richard and Clara Winston (New York: Harcourt, 1974), p. 3.

14. Ibid.

15. Ibid.

16. Ibid.

17. Ibid., p. 764.

18. Alain de Benoist, *Vue de droite* (Paris: Copernic, 1978), p. 556.

19. Fest, *Hitler*, p. 5.

20. Ibid., p. 5.

21. Speer, *Spandau: The Secret Diaries*, p. 80.

22. Steiner, *Portage to San Cristóbal*, p. 45.

23. Ernst Jünger, *Strahlungen* (Heliopolis Verlag, 1949), p. 322.

24. Interview with Michel Foucault, *Cahiers du cinéma*, nos. 251–52, July–August 1974, p. 10ff.

25. Ibid.

26. Ibid.

27. Pascal Bonitzer, "Le Secret derrière la porte," *Cahiers du cinéma*, nos. 251–52, July–August 1974, p. 33.

28. Steiner, *Portage to San Cristóbal*, pp. 44–45.

CHAPTER 3

1. Syberberg, *Hitler, a Film from Germany*, p. 3.

2. Serge Thion, *Vérité historique ou vérité politique? Le dossier de l'affaire Faurisson. La question des chambres à gaz (Historical or Political Truth? The Dossier of the Faurisson Affair. The Question of the Gas Chambers)* (Paris: La Vieille Taupe, 1980), p. 89.

3. Ibid., p. 179.

4. David Irving, *Hitler's War* (New York: Viking, 1977).

5. Hellmut Diwald, *Geschichte der Deutschen (History of the Germans)* (Frankfurt: Propyläen, 1978), p. 165.

6. Martin Broszat, "Hitler and the Genesis of the 'Final Solution,'" English translation in *Yad Veshem Studies*, 13(1979): 93–94.

7. George Steiner, *Language and Silence* (New York: Atheneum, 1970), pp. 123–24.

8. Ibid.

9. J. P. Stern, *History and Allegory in Thomas Mann's Doktor Faustus* (London, 1975), p. 92.

10. Sontag, *Under the Sign of Saturn*, p. 139.

11. Vincent Canby, "Free-Form Meditation, *New York Times*, 13 January 1980.

12. Steiner, *Language and Silence*, p. 7.

13. Ibid., p. 163.

14. David Stern, "Imagining the Holocaust," *Commentary*, July 1976, p. 49.

15. Syberberg, *Hitler, a Film from Germany*, pp. 60–61.

16. Tournier, *The Ogre*, p. 249.

17. Heinrich Himmler, speech of October 1943, International Military Tribunal at Nürnberg, vol. 29, doc. PS 1919, p. 145ff.

18. Maurice Bardèche, *Qu'est-ce que le fascisme?* (Paris: Les Sept Couleurs, 1970).

19. Steiner, *Portage to San Cristóbal*, p. 161.

20. Syberberg, *Hitler, a Film from Germany*, pp. 224–25.

21. Tournier, *The Ogre*, p. 581.

22. Steiner, *Portage to San Cristóbal*, pp. 162–63.

23. Ibid., p. 169.

24. George Steiner, "Who Do You Think You Are Kidding, Dr. Gilbert?" *London Times*, 11 March 1982.

25. Hyam Maccoby, "Steiner's Hitler," *Encounter*, May 1982, p. 34.

CHAPTER 4

1. Alan Bullock, *Hitler: A Study in Tyranny* (New York: Harper & Row, 1962), pp. 374–75.

2. Ernst Nolte, *The Three Faces of Fascism* (New York: Holt, Rinehart & Winston, 1966), p. 19.

3. Eberhard Jäckel, *Hitler, Sämtliche Aufzeichnungen, 1905–*

1924 (Hitler, Collected Writings, 1905–1924) (Stuttgart: Deutsche Verlags Anstalt, 1980).

4. Adolf Hitler, *Libres propos,* vol. 2, p. 347.

5. Théodore Adorno and Max Horkheimer, "Éléments de l'antisémitisme," in *La Dialectique de la raison. Fragments philosophiques* (Paris: Gallimard, 1974), p. 214.

6. Abram Leon, *The Jewish Question: A Marxist Interpretation* (New York: Pathfinder, 1970). p. 237.

7. Ibid., p. 239.

8. Liliana Cavani, letter to *le Monde,* 25 April 1974.

9. Marie Chaix, "le Fascisme à la mode," *Nouvel Observateur* 492 (April 1974): 49.

10. Siegfried Kracauer, *From Caligari to Hitler: A Psychological History of the German Film* (Princeton: Princeton University Press, 1971), p. 67.

11. Fest, *Hitler,* p. 517.

Grateful acknowledgment is made for permission to reprint:

Excerpt from "Hitler and the Genesis of the 'Final Solution,' " by Martin Broszat, first appeared in *Yad Vashem Studies,* Volume XIII, 1979 (Jerusalem). Reprinted by permission of Yad Vashem.

Excerpt from "Free-form Meditation," by Vincent Canby, January 13, 1980, The New York Times. Copyright © 1980 by The New York Times Company. Reprinted by permission.

Excerpts from *Hitler,* by Joachim C. Fest. Copyright © 1973 by Verlag Ullstein, English translation copyright © 1974 by Harcourt Brace Jovanovich, Inc. Reprinted by permission of Harcourt Brace Jovanovich, Inc.

Excerpts from *Under the Sign of Saturn,* by Susan Sontag. Copyright © 1972, 1973, 1975, 1976, 1978, 1980 by Susan Sontag. Reprinted by permission of Farrar, Straus and Giroux, Inc.

Excerpt from *Inside the Third Reich,* by Albert Speer. Translation copyright © 1970 by Macmillan Publishing Co., Inc. Excerpt from *Spandau: The Secret Diaries,* by Albert Speer. Translation copyright © 1976 by Macmillan Publishing Co., Inc. Reprinted by permission of Macmillan Publishing Co., Inc.

Excerpt from *Language and Silence: Essays on Language, Literature and the Inhuman,* by George Steiner. Copyright © 1967 by George Steiner. Reprinted by permission of Atheneum Publishers.

Excerpt from *The Portage to San Cristóbal of A.H.,* by George Steiner. Copyright © 1979, 1981 by George Steiner. Reprinted by permission of Simon & Schuster, Inc.

Excerpts from *Hitler: A Film from Germany,* by Hans-Jürgen Syberberg, translated by Joachim Neugroschel. Copyright © 1978 by Rowohlt Taschenbuch Verlag GmbH, Reinbek bei Hamburg. Translation copyright © 1982 by Farrar, Straus and Giroux, Inc.

Excerpt from *The Ogre,* by Michel Tournier. Translation by Barbara Bray copyright © 1972 by Doubleday & Company, Inc. Reprinted by permission of Doubleday & Company, Inc.